What's Stopping You? Being More Confident

Why Smart People Can Lack Confidence, and What You Can Do About It

Robert Kelsey

CAPSTONE

Cover design: Binary & The Brain

This edition first published 2013
© 2013 What's Stopping You Ltd
What's Stopping You? is a trademark of What's Stopping You Ltd?

Registered office
Capstone Publishing Ltd. (A Wiley Company), John Wiley and Sons Ltd, The Atrium,
Southern Gate, Chichester, West Sussex, PO19 8SQ, United Kingdom

For details of our global editorial offices, for customer services and for information
about how to apply for permission to reuse the copyright material in this book please
see our website at www.wiley.com.

Wiley publishes in a variety of print and electronic formats and by print-on-demand.
Some material included with standard print versions of this book may not be included
in e-books or in print-on-demand. If this book refers to media such as a CD or DVD
that is not included in the version you purchased, you may download this material at
http://booksupport.wiley.com. For more information about Wiley products, visit www.
wiley.com.

Designations used by companies to distinguish their products are often claimed as
trademarks. All brand names and product names used in this book and on its cover are
trade names, service marks, trademark or registered trademarks of their respective
owners. The publisher and the book are not associated with any product or vendor
mentioned in this book. None of the companies referenced within the book have
endorsed the book.

Limit of Liability/Disclaimer of Warranty: While the publisher and author have used
their best efforts in preparing this book, they make no representations or warranties
with the respect to the accuracy or completeness of the contents of this book and
specifically disclaim any implied warranties of merchantability or fitness for a
particular purpose. It is sold on the understanding that the publisher is not engaged in
rendering professional services and neither the publisher nor the author shall be liable
for damages arising herefrom. If professional advice or other expert assistance is
required, the services of a competent professional should be sought.

Library of Congress Cataloging-in-Publication Data

Kelsey, Robert, 1964–
   What's stopping you? Being more confident [electronic resource] : why smart people
can lack confidence, and what you can do about it / Robert Kelsey.
      1 online resource.
   Includes bibliographical references and index.
   Description based on print version record and CIP data provided by publisher;
resource not viewed.
   ISBN 978-0-85708-318-0 (pdf) – ISBN 978-0-85708-319-7 (epub) –
ISBN 978-0-85708-320-3 (mobi) – ISBN (invalid) 978-0-85708-309-8 (pbk)
1. Self-confidence.   2. Self-actualization (Psychology)   3. Confidence.   I. Title.
   BF575.S39
   158.1–dc23
                                                                        2012038854

A catalogue record for this book is available from the British Library.

ISBN 978-0-857-08309-8 (paperback)   ISBN 978-0-857-08320-3 (ebk)
ISBN 978-0-857-08319-7 (ebk)   ISBN 978-0-857-08318-0 (ebk)

Set in 10/13.5 pt Sabon by Toppan Best-set Premedia Limited

Printed in Great Britain by TJ International Ltd, Padstow, Cornwall, UK

'Confidence is the key to so much in life. In this book, Robert Kelsey shows readers how to grow their self-belief and so improve their chances of success. Everyone has moments of doubt – this practical and personal book can help remove those demons and boost morale. I recommend it strongly.'

Luke Johnson, RSA Chairman, *Financial Times* columnist and author of *Start It Up!*

'Robert Kelsey's combination of searing honesty and genuine curiosity about how our lives are shaped make for compelling reading, and his consistent message that we are in control of our journey is a welcome one. His books are like service stations on the motorway of life (without the stale buns) zoom past them at your peril.'

Fi Glover, multi-award-winning broadcast journalist and BBC radio presenter

'At last – a book about how to be confident written by someone who has struggled with it himself. Robert Kelsey's own experiences help him distil the essential lessons for making self-confidence a way of life.'

Roman Krznaric, author of *How to Find Fulfilling Work* and co-founder of The School of Life

'Not the usual snakeoil self-help salesmanship – Kelsey really could make a difference to you.'

Oliver James, author of *They F*** You Up!*

'Robert Kelsey has distilled the thinking of numerous acknowledged writers and added insights borne of his own experience, to produce an invaluable resource for anyone lacking confidence.'

John Caunt, author of *Boost Your Self-Esteem*

'If you want to stop talking and start doing, confidence is important. In this personal and readable book Robert Kelsey explores the roots of poor confidence – including his own – and why it can be so debilita   sight, he guides the rea   orward.'

Rich   *t Doing*

700040119502

To Lucy, George and Eddie

CONTENTS

INTRODUCTION

'Whether you think you can, or think you can't, you're right,' said US industrialist Henry Ford. This pithy maxim from the man that brought motoring to the masses observes the gulf that exists between high and low confidence, and the fact the resultant potential outcomes are so different the term 'chalk and cheese' seems inadequate. Venus and Mars, more like, though even here we're comparing two rocky and distant planets. How about Switzerland and Somalia, with the self-doubters condemned to life in a self-generated failed and piratical state?

Yet Ford's statement makes the stakes higher still. Far from being declared a failed state, the under-confident are being written off as such. Their poor self-beliefs mean they remain the personal embodiment of Somalia no matter what they do or how much they change their behaviour. This is a terrible conclusion. But is it true? Can Somalia ever hope to become Switzerland: a quietly confident, highly productive, contented and peaceful state, if a little finicky about cigarette butts and chewing gum? And can we as people become confident when once we were riven with doubt? Not according to Ford, it seems, because self-doubt and low confidence will lead us to incorrect evaluations – bringing forth poor judgement, terrible choices and, yes, self-fulfilling and disastrous behaviours that confirm and compound our poor confidence.

But immediately we think of Singapore: once a marshy and malarial island occupied by a few dozen locals, some Chinese immigrants and the odd gin-soaked Brit, and now a gleaming high-income hive. Then there's Costa Rica: a backwater jungle of the Spanish empire with no natural resources, and now a stable democracy in a neighbourhood noted for civil wars and unstable regimes. And what about Botswana: once a desert with warring tribesmen and now Africa's prosperous and democratic gem?

The confidence industry

So countries *can* become Switzerland, meaning that – as people – we can surely develop the confident attributes of those in the happy half of Ford's conundrum. Can't we? According to the self-help industry we can. There are mountains of books, DVDs, coaching courses, therapies and gizmos dedicated to banishing poor confidence. Hypnotism, acupuncture, yoga, pilates, meditation, even medication (legal or otherwise): all claim wonders when it comes to confidence. We can even have operations aimed at changing, removing or adding body parts – with no other outcome promised than improved confidence.

Yet none of it can move us permanently to the positive side of Ford's quote because they all make the same mistake of assuming we're no more than raw materials ripe for processing. We're a blank canvas, they consider, ready to be filled with their colourful (and admittedly useful) methodologies and prescriptions for a more confident future.

If only it were so. We're far from a blank canvas. The under-confident are filled with the agonizing and detailed images of painful memories. If a canvas, we'd be a Picasso-like contortion of humiliations, defeats and put-downs. Of lost battles and spurned opportunities. For the under-confident, the journey towards confidence doesn't begin at zero. It begins at minus one-hundred.

We are complex humans that are the sum of our experiences, which – for people with low confidence – are usually negative if not downright painful. Painting confidence onto such a distorted canvas is not a cure, in my view. It's a recipe for further confusion and distortion, as well as a potentially painful reckoning as we struggle and then fail to reconcile our past humiliations with the buoyant and strident instructions being propagated.

Confidence is not like an immunization jab. It isn't injected into us through fine prose and motivational exercises. Confidence comes – almost exclusively – from experience. From getting something right and – importantly – understanding the how and why of its correctness, thus making it replicable (what's known as self-efficacy). Confidence is also a personal tool box, mostly of positive and repeatable achievements but also of attributes learnt through trial and error. A box that can produce successful outcomes, but also one that can deal with unsuccessful outcomes. That can cope with setbacks without being knocked off-course. And one that can even accept the negative view of others while remaining focused on our own positive outcomes.

That said, if deep, sustainable confidence requires one thing it's self-knowledge. It's knowing what we're good at, and realizing and accepting why – including the fact that talent, as we shall see, may have little to do with it. But it's also to know what we're *not* good at, and to accept this and also understand why. Confidence is about trust, courage, optimism and resilience, although it's also about not being over-confident or arrogant. More than anything, confidence gives us the ability to act, although it also gives us the ability *not* to act. To speak but to know when silence is the better option. To offer praise and accept criticism. To be open to ideas and learning. And to be reasonable, fair, humble, charitable and empathetic.

Confidence is . . .

It's everything I'm not in other words – or, at least, wasn't. Indeed, my own story is one of distrust, cowardice, pessimism and weakness. Perhaps from birth or – as we shall see – more likely from early experience, mine was the script of the under-confident person:

a fate seemingly carved in stone from an early age – very much in line with Ford's prophesy. This was despite my mother's efforts at increasing my confidence. Enrolled in judo classes, or the Cub Scouts, or the village drama club: each time I'd look at the competence of those around me (colour banded in the case of judo) and assume such changes were beyond me. Each time, no sooner had I joined than I sought a way out, my poor confidence exacerbated by the experience.

Poor confidence led me to fail my 11-plus, to perform poorly in the rough secondary-modern turned comprehensive I attended – somehow managing to avoid the mediocre education on offer and fail the tough-gang acceptance test – and to screw up my first career as a building surveyor. I approached each experience with fear and misgiving, and with an inner belief that failure was the likely outcome. Of course, I soon proved myself right. No matter what the avenue, everyone seemed to be better than me: brainier, cooler, tougher, more popular.

Only now – having gained confidence (at least in one area) – can I look back and see things more clearly, perhaps also noticing some of the barriers. A big one was motivation. The poor educational fare on offer, the dull pastimes of exurban housing estates – even the humdrum pursuits of a surveyor in the featureless Essex marshes: nothing inspired me or aroused my desires to the point where I became determined to gain competence. Only once motivated towards something I truly desired would I develop the resilience to overcome the hurdles. This happened when taking A' Level history at evening classes, when doing a degree in politics and modern history at the University of Manchester and when finally winning a sustainable role as a journalist on a financially-focused magazine.

Yet on each occasion the doubts remained. My background – of poor confidence compounded by failed endeavours – reared up to undermine the achievement. At key moments, my confidence deserted me. It seemed brittle, temporary, somehow going against the grain and therefore easily refuted. And when it wasn't, my insecurities led to hubris that soon brought me down with a bump.

For instance, my 'success' as editor of a financial magazine eventually led to a job offer in an investment bank. I worked both here and in the US but my poor self-beliefs meant my shallow early competence gelled into a disabling ineptitude (not a great trait for a banker), which had me soon admitting defeat and retreating – sheltering in my earlier journalistic competence by writing a book about my experiences in New York. Yet the book's lukewarm reception left me reeling. Rather than see it as a strong first step as an author, I became convinced I'd utterly failed: a conviction that, as Ford correctly noted, fulfilled itself.

The truth about confidence

So, unlike many self-help authors (a good number of which are quoted in the pages ahead), I've lived with poor confidence throughout most of my adult life. Even now – with a 'successful' PR business under my belt, and as the author of the 'bestselling' *What's Stopping You?* (on fear of failure) – my under-confidence is easily triggered, perhaps in areas where I still feel less than capable. Every pitch meeting, every speech – even every telephone call from a client or chat with a journalist – rouses the inner demons and still occasionally produces the results I most fear. Even the descriptions of my achievements feel false (note the use of quote marks in the statements above), or temporary or somehow fraudulently acquired.

Which brings me to my motivation for this book. The under-confident need to be told the truth about confidence: what it is, what it isn't, how it's developed and – importantly – how it's sustained. Certainly, I've had to learn every step as if walking a tightrope. And still my footing feels unsure and I worry excessively about the gentlest breeze – perhaps over-reacting so that my grip is all the more threatened. Yet that's the point. It's a truth no

What's Stopping You? Being More Confident

high-fiving motivational guru can impart because until you've experienced the deep, gnawing, silent (but screaming), claustrophobic dread of poor confidence – and how it impacts your every utterance or encounter – you cannot hope to encourage a better outcome.

After all, Ford was speaking from the right side of his prediction, meaning he had little to offer those he'd condemned. That said, he was wrong. A more accurate maxim would finish: 'if you think you can't – you've got a lot of hard work ahead of you' – although I admit it has less of a ring to it.

What's Stopping You Being More Confident? *Poor confidence generates self-reinforcing behaviour that results in the under-confident feeling condemned to a life of low attainment. Yet confidence comes from positive experiences that can help create the self-knowledge required for sustainable confidence.*

PART ONE
Explaining Poor Confidence

PART ONE

Explaining Poor Confidence

1

SCRIPTS

No one gives you confidence. It's not a gift – perhaps bestowed by a guru or mentor, or even a higher power. And it's not innate. It's something *you* develop, almost from the day you're born. That said, significant others can play a major role in determining whether you develop strong confidence, or whether – like me – you become under-confident. Impatient parents, critical siblings, inept teachers: all can turn the impressionable and mouldable young child into someone lacking the basic tools for confidence (see Part Two). Yet this doesn't condemn us. It just means we have to develop the required attributes for confidence as adults. Of course, this is a deliberate endeavour and therefore a much harder pursuit. Nonetheless, confidence *can* be learnt.

Of the significant others I list, all three have a role in my story. Outwardly, mine was a normal upbringing in a typical 1960s-built exurban cul-de-sac on the edge of a 'village' (in fact a series of housing estates) in a dull Essex commuter town. My parents were typical of the area: two cars, two incomes, two children – in fact, doing rather nicely a generation on from their bombed-out East End heritage. Yet my family was divided. Dad played favourites, making my sister the apple of his eye: a position of power that confirmed my status as the 'annoying little brother'.

As we shall see, such a status provides the under-confident with their 'scripts' for life. Certainly, my script was written early on, with my mother's attempts at protecting me from both my father's and sister's disdain exaggerating the family divisions. These became a chasm when the family split, with my father and sister going to live in a different cul-de-sac in a different patchwork of housing estates.

Yet, within a year they were back. And the script (which had been temporarily converted into the 'uncontrollable tearaway') resumed, though with my crimes broadening to include relationships beyond the house. My sister's friends, local hardnuts keen to win her favours, even my peers at school, all took their cues from my family dynamic – furthering my self-doubt. Indeed, by my teens my poor confidence was deeply rooted: so deep that I failed to develop an awareness of social norms. In fact, I constantly transgressed norms – often generating poor reactions without even realizing why. I was personally inept and verbally clumsy, with each *faux pas* compounding my poor confidence.

Supports for poor confidence

Geography didn't help. Our cul-de-sac was away from the others in the village – a distance from the housing estates full of normal children happily playing together. I was constantly on the edge of the gang. I felt marginalized – an outsider. And this led to further problematic behaviour as I tried to ingratiate myself (including shop-lifting and minor vandalism). Soon the local mothers despised me, which meant I became defensive – rude even – and further isolated.

Yet my father remained the key figure, and the one sending the clearest signals of rejection. Doting on the eldest – especially a daughter – is perhaps an inevitable and therefore forgivable trait for a man with no siblings of his own and with a strained upbringing involving a five-year abandonment when evacuated. This may have made him resentful towards my childhood comforts, or he may have had an anachronistic view of discipline and boys (even for the 1970s). Whatever the cause, when contrasted with my sister's treatment, I look back and observe an emotional neglect that left me bewildered, paranoid and, of course, deeply lacking in confidence.

As for the teachers – they should have known better. This was not a deprived area, although my own difficulties revolved around the fact I favoured more creative pursuits and disliked formal learning, which the low-grade teachers couldn't accommodate – especially when the lessons seemed so geared towards the well-behaved girls.

In fact, as a late-July baby I was potentially two years educationally adrift from the brightest girls in the class. Constantly behind, I again developed behavioural issues that meant I became disliked by the teachers (who were also local and therefore in tune with the views of the village) – to the point where I was falsely blamed for more serious incidents of vandalism, with the inevitable results for my embattled self-esteem.

A life sentence

While a distressing story for a child, however, it hardly stacks up as a justification for a lifetime disabled by poor confidence. It even reads as a pathetic self-justification for low attainment: a grown man unable to escape the scripts of his childhood – condemned to remain a small boy that's forever trapped in a place where he's misunderstood, disliked and emotionally neglected. Where's the abuse, the violence, the war or poverty?

But normality is the narrative for most lives in Britain and other developed countries. And poor confidence is as much bred among the carpet and curtains of suburbia as the dirt and deprivation of poverty. We should all be happy and well-adjusted, shouldn't we? So if we're not – well – the fault must be ours, which only compounds the divide between the haves and have-nots when it comes to confidence: adding guilt, confusion and isolation to our fear and timidity.

While the confident excel, the under-confident flounder in a sea of insecurities – blamed for our misfortunes often by the very people who robbed us of our confidence. While we struggle to be understood, they fall back on platitudes such as 'get over it' or 'buck up' or 'you don't know how lucky you are': all of which add layers of self-loathing to our confirmed and deepening lack of confidence. While one group have their confidence constantly reaffirmed, the other have to suffer silently – with their doubts and uncertainty hidden or masked through avoidance tactics that can encompass a range of marginal behaviours.

We can become the swot or the giver – existing only to please others. Or we can be the rebel pretending not to care. Yet these are the better responses. Anger, depression, violence or deviant behaviour – all can mask deeply-held insecurities when it comes to confidence. Certainly, the under-confident suffer more anxiety and stress than their confident peers, and endure higher incidents of mental illness. They're also more likely to divorce (or never marry), be made redundant, drop out of education, become destitute, develop dependencies on drugs and alcohol, become overweight and therefore more prone to heart disease, smoke (making them more prone to cancer), have major accidents, commit suicide or be convicted of a crime. Their life is nastier – brutish even – and their life-expectancy shorter. Meanwhile, they have to live with the nagging guilt that, somehow, this is *their* fault and, therefore, no more than they deserve.

Being under-confident can feel like a life (and sometimes a death) sentence – and one unlikely to find release via the strident and dismissive maxims of the confident.

Replaying the scripts of childhood

Yet there is hope. As stated, there's nothing innate about confidence. We *can* change, although we first need to understand our condition. As shown by my own case, it's most likely the nuances of those early relationships that drive the gulf between those with and without confidence. Our confidence (or otherwise) is developed in the tiny power plays between parent and child, between siblings or peers, and between teacher and pupil. It's these early experiences that create the context for our later relationships, and just about everything else.

'How we react to our friends as well as who we pick as a lover, our abilities and interests at work, in fact almost everything about our psychology as an adult is continually reflecting our childhood in our day-to-day, moment-by-moment experience,' writes Oliver James in his widely acclaimed book on family survival called *They F*** You Up* (2002).

We live out the drama of our childhoods again and again – playing the same role, finding the same characters, forcing them (and ourselves) into the same responses: hence James' use of the word 'script' when describing these early power plays. Our scripts trap us, seemingly forever, on a destructive and dizzying round-about of triggered reactions – generating familiar results over and over until no relationship seems complete until it becomes aligned with our primary childhood dynamic.

My fear of rejection, my poor confidence with the opposite sex, my defensiveness with authority figures – and my propensity to see attack when there was only mild rebuke (or even positive advice) – all come from my early relationships with my father, my sister, my peers and those village-school teachers. Everyone I come into contact with plays one of those key roles: if not immediately, then eventually.

Same parents, different parenting

Of course, while conditioning is important, we also genetically inherit personality traits from our parents: don't we? Well, not according to James, who states that our personality is almost entirely influenced by our early experiences, *not* our genes.

'The pattern of electricity and chemistry which makes the thoughts and feelings in each person's brain unique is hugely influenced by the way that person was related to in early childhood,' he writes.

Using depression as an example he notes that 'if one's mother was depressed, the thoughts and feelings that this engendered become established as measurably different electro-chemical patterns in the frontal lobes of the right side of the brain. Psychologists know that these patterns are not inherited because they are absent at birth, and only show up if the mother behaves in a depressed fashion when relating to the child'.

James also states that the earlier these patterns are established the harder they are to shift, and that – of course – these psychological dysfunctions go far wider than depression: encompassing feelings of anxiety, stress, defensiveness and rejection (all cued up from those early relationships and experiences). And while experiences in our teenage years – and even adulthood – are also important, it's our first six years that set the pattern, says James, meaning that our personality is hardwired during the period we are least able to influence it.

Indeed, this would explain why I'm now so different to my sister. Although physically in the same house at the same time, we were brought up by different parents. My sister was daddy's girl, constantly being reassured by his love, while I was verbally and sometimes physically rejected. He was a quiet, measured and inwardly-assured man, which hugely influenced my sister who also became quiet, measured and inwardly assured. Meanwhile, I was noisy, erratic and under-confident – with the noise explained as the 'annoying little brother' vying for attention.

'Each parent treats each child so differently that they might as well have been raised in completely different families,' says James. 'Believe it or not, our uniqueness has far more to do with that than with our genes.'

Playing favourites

Recent support for this view comes from psychologist Jeffrey Kluger, author of *The Sibling Effect: What the Bonds Among Brothers and Sisters Reveal About Us* (2011).

'It's one of the worst-kept secrets of family life that all parents have a preferred son or daughter,' he says (in an article for *Time* magazine), 'and the rules for acknowledging it are the same everywhere: the favoured kids recognize their status and keep quiet about it . . . the unfavoured kids howl about it like wounded cats. And on pain of death, the parents deny it all.'

Kluger cites a study of 384 sibling pairs and parents undertaken by Catherine Conger at the University of California. Over three years she questioned them about their relationships and concluded that 65 percent of mothers and 70 percent of fathers exhibited a preference for one child, usually the older one.

'And those numbers are almost certainly lowballs,' says Kluger, 'since parents try especially hard to mask their preferences when a researcher is watching.'

According to Kluger, zoologists often observe favouritism among animals (again, usually towards the larger or older offspring), often with fatal consequences: penguins removing the smaller eggs in order to concentrate on the largest; eagles allowing the largest chick to eat the smaller ones – the examples go on and on.

'The function of the second chick is insurance,' says Douglas Mock, a professor of zoology at the University of Oklahoma (quoted by Kluger). 'If the first chick is healthy, the policy is cancelled.'

And the impact on confidence is obvious. Favoured children grow up with higher levels of self-esteem and therefore more confidence, with the reverse also true of less favoured siblings.

'Kids who feel less loved than another sibling have a higher risk of developing anxiety, depression and low-self-esteem,' says Kluger, with poor confidence its inevitable manifestation.

Winner takes all

Of course, it's not just favoured siblings or neglectful parents that provide the roots for poor confidence, although it's certainly a common cause. Being the fat kid, or the small kid, or the gangly ginger thick kid (or the swot, come to that): all can single us out at home or school or in the street as beyond the mainstream. We are the outcast – the specimen to be sacrificed when the food runs out or the boat sinks or the gods require it.

We may be terrible at sports (I was). We may be profoundly unmusical (that was also me). Or we may be poor at formal studies (yes, that too). In fact, we may have lacked *any* prop for developing childhood confidence – not least because our low confidence meant our view of skill acquisition was the opposite of the confident child's. They had confidence, so approached tasks in the expectation of acquiring the reward from learning new skills (praise being a key one). Meanwhile, the under-confident child assumes failure as the likely outcome from any attempt at skill acquisition (with humiliation the likely result), which leads us to behave in ways that make failure almost certain – largely because we look for ways of avoiding participation.

This is a winner-takes-all scenario, or more likely a loser-loses-all. It's also a contrivance that we *must* reverse if we're not to spend our entire lives in the purgatory of poor confidence. A poor confidence, what's more, that will potentially destroy our career prospects, disable our relationships (with peers, partners, seniors, juniors and even our children), erode our happiness, and wreck our well-being.

Confidence is the lifeblood of self-esteem: both its cause and a result. It therefore cannot be ignored by anyone reaching adulthood and thinking there's a deficit in this respect. It's something we *must* tackle – head on – if we're to avoid a life filled with foreboding, angst, disappointment, distress and sadness.

The underlying malaise – low-self-esteem

Of course, what's wrong is not poor confidence, which is just a symptom (although a crucial one). The underlying malaise is low self-esteem. And it's here we must start our journey towards redemption.

'If . . . you feel your true self to be weak, inadequate, inferior or lacking in some way,' writes Melanie Fennell in her bestselling book *Overcoming Low Self-Esteem* (1999), 'if you are troubled by uncertainty and self-doubt, if your thoughts about yourself are often unkind and critical, or if you have difficulty in feeling that you have any true worth or entitlement to the good things in life, these are the signs that your self-esteem is low. And low self-esteem may be having a painful and damaging effect on your life.'

Self-esteem is concerned with the judgements and evaluations we have of ourselves. We present these judgements as facts that brook no debate – that's just how we are, which results in us interpreting every event in our life as supporting evidence for our negative self-beliefs.

'Actually, however, they are more likely to be opinions than facts,' says Fennell. 'Summary statements or conclusions you have come to about yourself, based on the experiences you have had in your life, and in particular the message you have received about the kind of person you are.'

Of course, positive experiences – especially when young – lead to positive self-beliefs. Negative experiences, meanwhile, lead to negative self-beliefs. It's that simple, although the impact of each supposition couldn't be further apart.

'Negative self-beliefs about yourself constitute the essence of low self-esteem,' says Fennell. 'And this essence may have coloured and contaminated many aspects of your life.'

According John Caunt, author of *Boost Your Self-Esteem* (2002), low self-esteem can present itself in many ways:

- Doing things purely for the approval of others
- Constantly comparing yourself to others
- Resenting those that succeed
- Feeling like a failure
- Focusing purely on the negative (about yourself)

- Becoming upset by (even constructive) criticism
- Giving in to others' desires
- Not taking action from fear of failure and looking foolish
- Striving for unrealistic perfection
- Worrying excessively, but not asking for help
- Taking advantage of others – even bullying
- Putting others down and being abusive
- Putting yourself down – publicly and privately
- Feeling out of control and unable to make decisions
- Withdrawing into yourself and avoiding social events
- Becoming aggressive or even overly passive
- Becoming boastful or controlling
- Punishing yourself, or not allowing yourself to feel good.

And if some of these seem contradictory, it's because they are. It's the middle ground that causes problems for those with low self-esteem. For instance, Fennell agrees with Caunt that those with low self-esteem are often self-critical – even publicly – while also over-boastful when something does go well. It's quiet confidence that's missing: the inner knowledge that we are competent and therefore have no need to make public statements about our abilities or achievements.

Equally, we may be shy or withdrawn, but also pushy and self-promoting – with us potentially swinging between the two. Again, what's missing is the inner regulator: the person able to communicate effectively without crossing the social boundaries – indeed, knowing these boundaries exist and where they lie.

Sadness is also easily triggered by those with low self-esteem, which can quickly lead to depression (see Part Five). But equally – thanks to our poor emotional regulation – we can become elated, even overjoyed by a particular event. Low-self esteemers can also be fearful, shying away from risk. But we can then be foolhardy – happy to take ridiculous gambles (even with our personal safety) – because it's our assessment of risk that's the problem (as well as the value we put on our own well-being). Blame is another one. We absorb blame and are strong apologists (usually). Yet we can also blame others almost instantly. We think others conspire against us, but can also be far too trusting – often investing faith too readily, even in objects or mysticism. We can be fiercely loyal, but also too critical; poorly behaved, but also very moralistic; wildly generous, but habitually mean; empathetic, but also cruel.

In short, for those with low self-esteem, it's our evaluation that's gone awry. We have poor judgement and therefore no ability to regulate our feelings, our reactions and even our thoughts. No wonder our confidence is shot.

The development and maintenance of low self-esteem

Fennell helpfully breaks low self-esteem into two parts: how it develops (usually in childhood) and how it's maintained (usually in adulthood). She describes the following dynamic for development:

- *Early experiences*: events and relationships that engender ideas about 'self' such as rejection, neglect or being the 'odd one out' – which lead to . . .
- *The bottom line*: an assessment of our worth or value as a person, including feelings such as 'I am worthless' and 'I am just not good enough' – which leads to . . .
- *Rules for living*: guidelines for coping or survival, such as 'I must avoid this', or 'I must always put others first' or 'if I am myself I will be rejected' – which leads to . . .
- *Trigger situations*: in which the rules for living are transgressed, resulting in feelings of rejection or failure, or of being out of control.

Yet such a dynamic needs to be maintained via a self-supporting mechanism, which Fennell plots thus:

- Activation of our feelings of worthlessness (our bottom line), leading to . . .
- Negative predictions, leading to . . .
- Anxiety or unhelpful behaviour (such as avoidance or disruption), leading to . . .
- Confirmation of the bottom line, leading to . . .
- Self-critical thoughts, leading to . . .
- Depression, which (again) activates the bottom line.

Those early experiences have not only remained unchallenged into adulthood, they have generated a self-reinforcing and therefore self-fulfilling mechanism that's regularly triggered – generating a seemingly-unstoppable vortex of destruction for the under-confident person.

Sound familiar? It certainly did for me. My early-life experiences set the course until my late 30s when I finally decided to seek professional help. But as both Fennell and James point out, low self-esteem is a learnt condition. There's nothing genetic about it – it's hardwired into us from our first breaths. Indeed, James goes to some length to refute those famed 1990s studies into similarities in personality found in twins separated at birth (which suggest genetically-based personality traits) – even going as far as suggesting the research was funded by pro-eugenics agencies that advocate racial differences. Certainly, more recent studies (including those analyzing the impact of trauma while in the womb) back up James' thesis that, when it comes to our personalities and especially our outlook on life, it's conditioning that matters, not genes.

Self-esteem is a journey not a destination

Genes or otherwise, it *is* hardwired. So can our low self-esteem – and therefore our poor confidence – be undone? Is a rewiring possible? What matters, it seems, is not the final destination but the direction of travel. There's no moment when you'll wake up shouting *'eureka, I'm cured'*, not least because such feelings could be a sign of hubris (see Part Five). Start heading towards a more positive place, however, and you immediately reverse the self-fulfilling negativity of low self-esteem, whether you end up at a destination called *High Self-esteem* or not. And the realization that your genes are not responsible – you developed these beliefs and responses from negative experiences – can help you to switch trajectories.

It's depressing to realize that, in part, we did this to ourselves. But it's also a liberating thought. In fact, it's a fantastic moment because it confirms that *nothing* is ordained. We're not condemned to this path. We learnt this when we were helpless and can therefore learn something new now we're more capable. Sure, some of the damage might be permanent. But less than we think, not least because our self-knowledge regarding how we got here means we can stop adding to the damage. In fact, we can start undoing some of the harm right away.

What's Stopping You Being More Confident? *Confidence is something you develop from birth based on your relationship scripts, which can condemn you to a life playing the same role. The underlying malaise is low self-esteem. No sustainable instant cure is available but you can reverse the direction of travel.*

2

MINDSET

If self-esteem is a direction of travel rather than a destination, confidence is no more than one of the tools we use for the journey. Yet there's something inadequate about the 'never-ending journey' – something off-putting for under-confident people who'll want to strive towards a more tangible objective than overcoming a seemingly-incurable condition. And it's here where the concept of self-actualization can help.

Self-actualization is 'the desire for self-fulfilment', writes Abraham Maslow, one of the more famous psychologists propagating self-actualization as a key human endeavour, 'namely the tendency for [the individual] to become actualized in what he is potentially . . . to become everything that one is capable of becoming'.

Of course, such a quest requires us to differentiate because we cannot reach our full potential in everything. Differentiation is for later, however (see Part Three). At this point we simply need to accept self-actualization as an objective. Indeed, according to psychologists such as Maslow, it's as hardwired into us as our instincts for survival and reproduction (although philosophical arguments abound regarding the 'teleological' – i.e. goal-seeking – nature of the human animal).

Hierarchy of needs

The desire for self-actualization is, therefore, an important concept for the under-confident to grasp, because only then can we understand the role confidence plays on that journey, as well as why we may have struggled to acquire it. And it's here where Maslow explains self-actualization using his famous 'hierarchy of needs'. As described in his ground-breaking essay *A Theory of Human Motivation* (1943), Maslow's hierarchy plots our path towards self-actualization, where the lower needs *must* to be met prior to gaining access to the next level, with self-actualization the ultimate goal.

The hierarchy is usually expressed as a pyramid with the lowest level made up of basic needs such as breathing, food and water. Only once these are satisfied will we seek the next level – labelled 'safety' – in which we require security, health and employment. With these acquired, it's up to the next level of 'love and belonging', where our needs include the desire for friendship, family and intimacy.

Yet we still have work to do to reach our 'actualized' self. 'Esteem' comes next, which brings us needs such as *confidence*, achievement and recognition or respect from others. And this delivers us to the 'self-actualization' summit, where we indulge such high-order concerns as morality and creativity, as well as reap beneficial traits such as a lack of prejudice as well as empathy and charity (what Maslow termed 'self-transcendence' or a desire to move beyond oneself having seemingly achieved *self-*actualization).

For those seeking confidence, this is such an important explanatory concept it bears repeating:

- *Self-actualization.* Charity, creativity, morality, lack of prejudice – is sought once we have . . .
- *Esteem.* Confidence, achievement, recognition – is sought once we have . . .

- *Love and belonging.* Friendship, family, intimacy – is sought once we have . . .
- *Safety.* Security, health, employment – is sought once we have . . .
- *Basic needs.* Food, water, air etc.

For those seeking confidence and self-esteem, Maslow's hierarchy is a wonderfully-graphic illustration of both the purpose of confidence – as a milestone requirement for reaching our full self-actualized potential – and the true reason we have *not* gained confidence: having failed to reach the 'esteem' level on Maslow's pyramid due to our inability to satisfy the lower needs of 'love and belonging'. Maslow's view is that high self-esteem and strong confidence will elude us until we have satisfied our requirements with respect to our sense of belonging as well as the support that comes from feeling loved.

Maslow confirms it: those early-life scripts are suppressing our confidence in adulthood.

Flaws with Maslow

Discovering Maslow's simple hierarchy was one of those powerfully-enlightening moments for me. Sure, life is more nuanced than this. There's always the detailed exceptions to trip up such generalizations. Yet the clarity of Maslow's description, as well as the prescriptive power of the pyramid (and my own position on it) bowled me over. There I sat, languishing at the 'love and belonging' level, wondering why strong confidence eluded me when the answer was simple: how could I be confident when I was still struggling to be loved? Without love and belonging, confidence and self-esteem are impossible. Just as obviously, without self-esteem and confidence, I would be incapable of expressing myself creatively (or morally come to that).

Yet, soon enough, the flaws in Maslow's pyramid begin to show. A major one is the 'tortured genius'. Many of history's greatest men and women suffered low self-esteem – dismissing their own achievements through self-doubt and self-hatred, often suffering depression or even suicidal thoughts as a result. It's even possible to conclude that their great works came about *only* as a result of their insecurities. Surely they have somehow corrupted Maslow's hierarchy?

Indeed, they have. Yet the Van Gogh's of this world are the noisy exceptions. And, who knows, perhaps – at the 'genius' level of attainment – such doubts are inevitable (although Part Two reveals more on the true nature of talent and genius). For mere mortals, however, self-actualization is a product of self-esteem, which – in turn – is a product of love and belonging (which requires a strong sense of security). And this means Maslow's path works well as a benchmark for our progress.

The safety trap

There's another concern to inject into Maslow's thesis, however – and one with more serious consequences for anyone seeking confidence. Our assumption that we remain stuck at the 'love and belonging' level may be wrong. From childhood experiences, we may still be concerned with safety, which will render us incapable of graduating to the 'love and belonging' level (let alone to the point where we can develop our 'esteem').

'Some neurotic adults in our society are, in many ways, like the unsafe child in their desire for safety,' writes Maslow. 'Their reaction is often to unknown psychological dangers in a world that is perceived to be hostile, overwhelming and threatening. Such a person behaves as if a great catastrophe were almost always impending, i.e., he is usually responding to an emergency.'

Certainly, I recognize myself in the above description – constantly fearing disaster, I can almost feel relieved when the predicted disaster is upon me (allowing me a 'told you so' satisfaction), denying the fact the 'disaster' could be self-fulfilling or even illusionary.

Yet, according to Maslow, this is a reflection of the fears generated in those formative years – making us incapable of a strong sense of belonging or of being loved. And while, for me, marriage and a degree of economic security have changed this, those insecurity scripts still play out when triggered.

'A neurotic adult may be said to behave "as if" he were actually afraid of a spanking, or of his mother's disapproval, or of being abandoned by his parents, or having food taken away from him,' says Maslow, who adds that these reactions to such dangers may have been 'untouched' by reaching adulthood.

In this environment, we have to first establish security. Only once 'safe' can we develop the sense of belonging that would encourage our confidence and self-esteem. Maslow even points to those with a compulsive-obsessive neurosis – opining that they are frantically trying to 'order and stabilize the world so that no unmanageable, unexpected or unfamiliar dangers will ever appear'.

Equally, those that cling too deeply to religion or mysticism or some other external focus offering order in a chaotic and dangerous world are – according to Maslow – trying to satisfy their needs for safety and security, often thanks to an upbringing devoid of such comforts.

Trauma-based therapies

Does this mean we're condemned by our insecurities – never to rise up the ranks of Maslow's hierarchy because it's impossible to go back to those early years and force a better outcome? Well there is Primal Therapy – a trauma-based psychotherapy based on using hypnosis to fully re-experience repressed pain from our childhood in order to express the resulting pain in adulthood.

According to its founder Arthur Janov, by bringing the pain to the surface we can access parts of the central nervous system that 'talking therapies' (as he and others call them) cannot – a process that allows us to resolve the pain through 'complete processing and integration'. The pain becomes real and apparent – rather than repressed and unconscious. And that means it can now be dealt with openly, which – over time – should lessen the hold the early trauma exerts in adult life.

Of course, this sounds wonderful in theory – the wished-for rewiring that so many insecure people crave once they recognize their condition and understand its root cause. Yet Primal Therapy has been dismissed in more mainstream psychological circles: criticized for being shallow, trendy (John Lennon and Yoko Ono were reportedly followers) and infantile, as well as relying on the power of suggestion (similar to past-life hypnosis) and irrefutability (i.e. constructed in a way that prevents it being disproved).

A better way to tackle the genuine pain of childhood trauma, in my opinion, is to accept it as part of our history. Like a war-torn country, we cannot go back in time and hope to avoid the mistakes that led to the war. We can only acknowledge the war as a historical fact, use it as a learning tool and – with the acute awareness that comes from such a tragic experience – leverage the self-knowledge it gives us to our advantage.

The growth mindset

Indeed, while you cannot change who you are or what has happened to you, you *can* change your future. Nothing is ordained. The future remains unwritten, although we need to adopt the right *mindset* in order to both realize this and to tackle it constructively.

'The view that you adopt for yourself profoundly affects the way you lead your life,' writes Carol Dweck, Stanford University psychologist and author of the hugely influential book *Mindset* (2006).

Dweck's thesis states that, for years, experts have attributed people's differences in outlook, motivation and skill acquisition to an individual's environment, physiology and genes. Yet there's another factor that, for her, is far more important: whether we have a 'fixed' or 'growth' mindset. And while most people believe their attributes are fixed (perhaps by their genes), for Dweck this simply means they have a fixed mindset – that they consider their personality or intelligence predetermined (or at least hardwired in early life) and therefore unshakable. Meanwhile, others believe they can improve or change their personal characteristics, including their intelligence, over time and through learning and practice. According to Dweck, these people have a growth mindset. And from such a mindset springs sustainable confidence and plausible self-esteem.

In my view, this revolutionary way of viewing attainment is of enormous help to the under-confident looking for a way out of their mental prison. Dweck doesn't ask us to deny our past pain, or its impact. She doesn't even ask that we pursue confidence as our goal. She simply asks us to reorient our thinking towards seeking growth (and therefore learning) rather than constantly seeking proof of our attributes (or otherwise), which will lead us to either accept our apparently-fixed attributes or to try and hide them.

According to Dweck, people with growth mindsets believe:

• That through learning, they can change
• That they can acquire or build talents through practice
• That failures and setbacks are learning tools
• That winning is important but it's part of a process not a destination (making losing also important).

Dweck illustrates her claim by asking us to consider the reactions to students achieving a C+ in an exam on the same day they received a parking ticket (two mildly negative but unrelated events for those wealthy Californian school children driving to High School). Those with fixed mindsets link the two negatives – using statements such as 'everyone is better than me' or 'I'm a total failure' or even 'the world is out to get me'. Those with growth mindsets, meanwhile, respond by saying they'll work harder and park more carefully.

'You don't have to have one mindset or the other to be upset,' says Dweck. 'Yet those people with the growth mindset were not labelling themselves or throwing up their hands . . . they were ready to take the risks, confront the challenges and keep working on them.'

You are work-in-progress

Dweck's concept is a liberating one for the under-confident, although some may initially react negatively – perhaps concluding they have a fixed mindset. Yet their potential anxieties about developing a growth mindset may be overblown. After all, you picked up this book, and even got this far. So there's clearly a growth mindset in there that perhaps became fixed from all the negative feedback you received as a child.

That said, literally within the space of reading this sentence, you can switch from a fixed mindset – in which you assume you're as you are – to a growth mindset, in which you assume that you have it *all* to learn. Of course, such a revelation will need constant reinforcement – and your new mindset will be challenged by every setback. Yet the realization that you're nothing more than *work-in-progress* – and that this is good news because self-actualization requires a growth mindset – is a sustainable one in my view. Certainly, having realized this obvious truth – that continuous learning is not only possible but a must for your future progress – you're in a far stronger position than you were, even at the beginning of this paragraph.

Still not convinced? OK, I'll confess my own previously-fixed mindset, and how it still occasionally corrupts my thinking:

- I can spend too much time looking to prove my intelligence. At times, I consider this more important than being effective in communication and certainly more important than listening.
- In fact, I can look for external reinforcement for all my actions. This was once from my mother (perhaps because it was withheld by my father) and is now from my wife, colleagues and clients. In time, I expect it will be from my children.
- To this day, my instant reaction to failure is as a confirmation of my inner beliefs regarding my limited capacity in a particular area (in fact most areas). For me, failure doesn't signal a skill to be learnt but a potential humiliation to be avoided – something I have to force myself to rethink.
- I can be very challenged by change – fearful, even. I hate moving house or office, holidays make me anxious and I fear aging. In fact, as I age, my feelings in this respect harden to the point where it cripples decision-making: on investments or partnerships for example.

Of course, I've also learnt to challenge my mindset – to force it in a different direction. Certainly, it's the growth mindset that helped me calculate my goals (and made me realize the need for goal-setting). It's also the growth mindset that forces me to learn new skills or acquire new knowledge, because such pursuits help me move towards my goals. And it's the growth mindset that keeps me going – and learning – even when I experience setbacks or outright failures: over-riding my underlying desire to quit.

'The passion for stretching yourself and sticking to it, even (or especially) when it's not going well, is the hallmark of the growth mindset,' says Dweck.

If you've a growth mindset you're literally starting every day focusing, not on who you are, but on what you can learn. This is a blank piece of paper that you can fill as you please. You don't need to be hampered by the past, although you do need to think about – and plan for – the future (see Part Three).

Gaining confidence requires a growth mindset

And, crucially, with the growth mindset you've overcome what you thought was your biggest obstacle to progress: your poor confidence. In fact, Dweck reverses the suggestion that those with a fixed mindset simply lack confidence – stating that it's your mindset that determines whether you lose or gain confidence.

She cites computer-training experiments by Joseph Martocchio in which half the class were pre-warned that acquiring computer literacy required an innate ability, while the other half were told the crucial need was lots and lots of practice. By the end of the course, those offered the growth-mindset advice – that it required practice – had gained considerable confidence in their computer skills, and continued to learn after the course. Meanwhile, those offered the fixed-mindset prophesy not only struggled from the off, but lost confidence as the course progressed.

Could it be that confidence is therefore not the acquisition of skills or excellence in a particular area? Is it, instead, our openness to the fact we're not perfect, yet feel the journey towards perfection worthwhile nonetheless? Growth and confidence are therefore aligned, which also means there's a dangerous trap awaiting those arriving at the top of Maslow's pyramid: if you assume you've achieved self-actualized perfection (meaning you have total confidence in a particular area), you clearly have a fixed mindset, with hubris and humiliation the likely result (see Part Five).

Mindset transcends confidence

That said, Dweck is at pains to point out that mindset transcends the concept of confidence.

'In the growth mindset you don't always need confidence,' says Dweck, you simply need the desire to grow.

This is a fantastically-liberating thought for those struggling to make progress – and usually blaming their poor confidence for the setbacks. Struggle – in whatever respect – simply alerts you to the fact you're at the beginning of the learning process.

'Even when you think you're not good at something, you can still plunge into it wholeheartedly and stick to it,' adds Dweck.

In fact, this is probably the most wonderful feature of the growth mindset – that we don't have to think we're good at something in order to enjoy doing it. The desire for growth is the key.

Of course, this works for positive events, such as acquiring a new sporting interest. But can it work for negative events, such as losing a job? According to Dweck, yes. Sure, we'll first focus on the emotions of being fired (or in other ways rejected), which is hardly enjoyable. But we can then ask ourselves what we learnt from the experience, and how we can use this learning as the basis for future growth.

This may be difficult during the maelstrom, because we're injecting an impossibly-rational evaluation into an emotionally-charged situation. Yet once the initial emotions dissipate it should become our focus. It should also be the evaluation we carry into the future. And knowing that – in time – this is how we *must* react to such an event should help bring that moment forward, which is a far better result than our more typical route of waiting years for the lesson to sink in, usually after further negative reinforcement.

Yet there's one more enormous benefit to having a growth mindset, in my view. Get this right and we could even end up thanking those we perceive as our early-life tormentors. They've given us the opportunity to fully understand our own psyche – how it impacts our inner motivations and our responses to others. And it's allowed us to consciously take steps towards a better, more directed, growth-filled and, indeed, self-actualized future, which is probably the best result anybody – confident or otherwise – could have hoped for.

What's Stopping You Being More Confident? *Confidence is a milestone towards self-actualization, although is only possible once you have found love and a sense of belonging (which requires safety). A key attribute is a 'growth mindset' in which you must accept that nothing is fixed and that life is about learning.*

3

REACTIONS

Changing our mindset is clearly not enough. After all, it's easy to make bland statements full of intent about our desire for growth. Sustaining it through years of setbacks and frustrations (that reinforce our negative or fixed beliefs) is a far more difficult task. Removing a lifetime of poor confidence – as well as its impact on our self-esteem (and *vice versa*) – is a major undertaking, I'm afraid, and one that no single book can deliver. Indeed, telling the embattled under-confident person to change their mindset can sound little better than the 'get over it' admonishments of the super-confident.

One issue is our reactions to such statements, or, indeed, to other moments when we feel challenged. The world of the under-confident person is one of reactivity, perhaps leading to timidity and withdrawal, but also leading to defensiveness – even anger. These are emotion-driven responses. And, in all cases, they're a disaster.

Too often it's those instant reactions that anchor the under-confident to the floor of their own insecurities. Certainly, on many mornings I've left home feeling 'up', only for an irritable email from a client or grumpy response from a colleague to throw my progress into reverse, and for my confidence to collapse. These are the moments when our veneer disappears and what we consider the real – under-confident – person re-emerges. It's like a game of snakes and ladders, with every snake taking us right back to the beginning.

CBT and self-beliefs

And it's here where cognitive behavioural therapy (CBT) can take a role. At heart, CBT recognizes that our self-beliefs generate patterns of thoughts that lead to, perhaps self-fulfilling, reactions. For instance, if someone blanks you in the street, you might assume that you're disliked by that person and avoid them. Equally, you could assume they were distracted and, concerned for their well-being, contact them – the two opposing reactions being dictated by our negative or positive self-beliefs. CBT aims to recognize these patterns and replace 'errors in thinking' – such as generalizing, magnifying negatives and 'catastrophizing' (see below) – with more realistic and less destructive thoughts and reactions.

Aaron Temkin Beck (a psychiatrist at the University of Pennsylvania) is widely accredited with the creation of CBT. Beck married cognitive therapy, which deals with dysfunctional thinking, and behaviour therapy, which aims to eliminate the negative responses that can lead to problematic behaviour. These two therapeutic traditions have one thing in common, claims Beck: they are both more concerned with the 'here and now' than the Freudian focus on our past, and particularly our childhood (see 'What the psychologists say' at the back of this book for more on various relevant psychologists).

It's this focus on our current reactions that makes CBT useful when trying to build confidence in the previously under-confident, especially when dealing with those instant responses.

'While [Sigmund] Freud's methods emphasized the importance of unpacking repressed conflicts from the past,' writes Dr Stephen Briers in *Brilliant Cognitive Behavioural Therapy* (2009), 'Beck became convinced that for many of his patients the crux of their problems lay more in what they were telling themselves in the present.'

Our characteristic style of thinking

As we have now seen, an examination of past behaviour can be wonderfully explanatory – peeling back the layers that have built and then confirmed negative self-beliefs. But it offers no way out, and can – in fact – trap us in the past: constantly reliving lost battles in the hope of achieving a better result (which, of course, is impossible).

As with the scripts described by Oliver James in Chapter One, Beck noticed that – whatever their origin – anxiety-laden commentaries inside his patients' heads were driving their emotions and reactions *now*. These could be no more than fleeting thoughts, but it was this 'characteristic thinking style' that dominated their current evaluations and generated their (usually negative or defensive) reactions. And this led Beck to promote 'healthier' thoughts that could challenge the negative and debilitating inner-voice of his patients.

CBT has since become the world's most widely-applied psychotherapy – utilized by both professionals and individuals seeking answers to their esteem, anxiety or confidence-related disorders. Even the NHS is a major advocate – with plans to train up to 10,000 therapists to work in 250 centres across the UK – not least because, according to its devotees, the basic principles can be mastered after just a few sessions (perhaps just one), rather than the lengthy unravelling required from traditional therapy.

That said, this is no instant cure.

'CBT is not a quick fix or magic wand,' says Briers. 'It will only work if you persevere. Busy schedules and frantic lifestyles can make it hard to get the most out of the techniques so be prepared to make some room in your life to do your homework.'

It will also only work if you're prepared to challenge every preconception you've held until now: about you, about others, and about the world around you. Every conviction must be re-examined, which – as Briers states – can be exciting but also unsettling.

'We are often strongly invested in our assumptions about things,' writes Briers, 'even if those assumptions aren't helping us. The beliefs that are the most rigid are often the ones that hold us back, and if you are the kind of person that has to win every argument, sees things in black and white, or always has to have the last word, then CBT may be quite challenging for you.'

CBT requires you to face yourself – warts and all. Yet this is more than having the ability to simply beat yourself up, which most under-confident people excel at. It's about the ability to challenge the assumptions behind your sometimes confused and emotion-laden thinking – the very thinking, in fact, that generates those horrible instant reactions.

The principles of CBT

In a book aimed at covering a lot of confidence-related ground, it's difficult to do full justice to the concepts that underpin CBT. That said, Briers has helpfully broken CBT down into the following five key principles.

Principle One: There is always another point of view
All humans are more than capable of receiving the same information in different ways, meaning that the interpretation *we* put on 'facts' can be wildly different from the interpretation someone else puts on the same information. We see this in politics – when two people (and even two parties) can look at the same event in entirely different ways. They may accuse the other of lying, but it's far more likely they simply have a different perspective, which is a major function of our conditioning.

CBT simply asks us to recognize this – perhaps injecting doubt into our previously-*fixed* view of a place, situation or person. If we recognize that there's no such thing as 'truth' – there's only perception and perspective – we should be in a better place to challenge our wholly-negative assumptions regarding events and even our place in the world. And this should improve our reactions. We're not being challenged or attacked: we're simply being exposed to a different perspective (certainly something I need reminding of occasionally).

Principle Two: Events don't cause our feelings

Just as perceptions of the same event can differ, so can our reactions to an event. Some may shrug off a minor accident or mishap or even a snub from a friend or colleague, while others will view it as confirmation of their un-likability or low status or poor luck (or all three). More importantly, some will rationalize events (both good and bad) as part of the cut-and-thrust of life, while others will react emotionally: feeling elated by positive events and upset and even depressed by negative events – perhaps trying to replace negative events with positive, rather than see the irrationality in both reactions.

According to CBT, this is due to the fact we're interpreting events based on our preconceptions. The feelings we experience from an event are, therefore, not based on the event but on the fact we're running the event along a script that we've assigned ourselves – again, most likely through early conditioning (although continually confirmed by our current thinking). If negative, the event is probably confirmation of our low status. If positive the event is perhaps 'deserved' because of all the pain we've previously experienced or may even be 'undeserved', which means we may assume there's a 'price' to be paid (usually a negative rebalancing).

Briers offers the example of a single man waiting for his date to arrive, who's running late. He could view it as a rejection, of course. Or he could view it as a verdict on women in general: perhaps that 'they cannot be trusted'. But he could also assume there's an explanation such as the traffic or that she's been held up at work, or is perhaps waiting at the wrong place. Of course, each reaction generates a different emotion (sadness, anger, concern, etc.). Yet it's his interpretation of the event – and therefore his reaction to the only known fact (that she's yet to greet him) – that's generated the emotions, not the event itself.

At least until more facts are known, the man has a choice regarding which interpretation he chooses – if any – as well as his reaction to that interpretation.

Principle Three: We all evolve characteristic ways of seeing the world
Much of the thinking responsible for these unwanted emotions is involuntary. These are what Beck calls Negative Automatic Thoughts (NATs) – the 'upsetting thoughts [that] simply pop into our heads unbidden', as Briers terms it.

Yet these unwanted emotions were learnt by us, and became entrenched – perhaps when we were in our helpless early years. And, according to CBT therapists, they can be unlearnt. This is the behavioural element of CBT, which borrows from the behaviourist school of psychology. Events shape us, say the behaviourists, because our brains search for patterns and draw conclusions based on the patterns found. If a child burns his or her hand on a stove, for instance, he or she will in future avoid both that stove and any like it.

'His internal model of the world has been updated,' says Briers – and while it's a generalized response (assuming all stoves are dangerous based on one negative incident), it's a useful one for the child's future safety.

'Emotional learning is no different,' says Briers. 'A child who is neglected or abused may instinctively generate theories or even reach hard and fast conclusions about herself and the world around her', including that she may also be abused by others or that grown-ups are bad people.

Over time, these views harden into core beliefs that are the 'bedrock of our internal working model of the world and are usually strongly resistant (but not impossible) to change,' says Briers.

Principle Four: It's a two-way street (or, our reactions can reinforce our beliefs)
If we become nervous walking down a particular street at night, our body will respond in ways that – driven by self-preservation – heighten our concern. Adrenaline will flow, we will become edgy and our attention will focus on unfamiliar sights and sounds – perhaps applying a more sinister interpretation. We could even panic and flee, thus confirming our fears when – in reality – nothing out of the ordinary has happened.

Once 'safe', our irrational self-confirming response should become apparent: we did nothing more than spook ourselves. Yet there are many occasions when we react in such self-confirming ways without our irrationality ever becoming apparent – perhaps when we react defensively towards someone else based on our perception of their view of us (or our view of them). Their response may, indeed, confirm our prejudices, although may have been their natural and forgivable reaction based on our prejudicial approach.

A classic for me in this respect is poor service in a shop or restaurant, which I immediately run through a negative script that assumes they're judging me personally – that I'm not worthy of good service, perhaps due to snobbery on their part. Of course, I respond defensively, which causes them to behave in ways that confirm my view. By assuming the worst, the worst – indeed – happens, which is the horrible self-fulfilling vortex of destruction that can be the life sentence of under-confident people.

Principle Five: We are all scientists at heart (or, we all seek generalized explanations)
'We are theory-building creatures,' says Briers. 'We can't help ourselves. We are constantly generating hypotheses about ourselves and the world, often without being aware that we are doing so.'

And while explaining how the world is (as we see it), our theories may have been unhelpful – offering a distorted and negative view that harms our self-esteem and destroys our confidence. So why not develop new ones that do the opposite?

Certainly, CBT relies on the fact we're not unreasonable people and can therefore accommodate new beliefs, which include the fact we may have been distorting events in our mind in order to uphold existing beliefs, as well as the notion that new information should allow new beliefs to form.

The exposure technique

Of course, understanding and challenging negative thought patterns that lead to poor reactions is all well and good, but can CBT offer anything specific for those seeking confidence? According to Corinne Sweet in *Change Your Life with CBT* (2010), yes.

'In fact, it is relatively easy to boost your confidence the CBT way,' she claims. 'It is all about recognizing the things you already do, and building on them.'

Sweet uses the example of becoming a confident driver, where we first sit in the driver's seat, becoming comfortable with handling the steering wheel and working out what the dashboard is telling us. This can be followed by starting the engine, or driving a small distance (with an instructor of course!) – all what Sweet calls the 'exposure technique'.

'Confidence building is just that,' says Sweet. 'Each time you do something you will learn that you are more capable, and more able, than you realize.'

Expecting to be immediately confident at something – anything – is a ridiculous notion based on poor self-beliefs and a fixed mindset. While others may pick up a new skill more quickly than you, they may have had a stronger grounding via the 'exposure technique' (often without realizing it), making them immediately several steps ahead. This doesn't make them innately more capable than you, just further along the learning curve,; although your self-beliefs that – indeed – they are more capable can become self-fulfilling.

Ingredients for change

Sweet states that we require three key ingredients to use CBT effectively for building confidence (with some thoughts of my own):

Overcoming the 'Change Paradox'
The change paradox states that, while accepting the need for change – even outwardly adopting a desire for change – many people hesitate when it comes to actual change, the paradox being that we want to change as long as we don't have to change anything. Indeed, routines are based on offering comfort and safety, so any change in routine is bound to make us uncomfortable and feel insecure.

Yet change occurs all the time, which means we should not resist change (because we fear it) but embrace it through good planning and positive pursuits (see Part Three). Viewing change negatively is the first step towards ensuring that the changes that occur are both out of our control – because we have tried to resist or avoid them – and, therefore, negative.

Self-acceptance
Another paradox. How can we embrace change and also accept ourselves for who we are? Surely, being under-confident is a recipe for disliking ourselves, or even becoming angry and depressed about who we are? And isn't feeling compelled to change the one upside of this negative self-view?

Yes, absolutely. But self-acceptance and a growth mindset are not only travelling in the same direction, they're fellow passengers. We're accepting ourselves for who we are but also accepting our capacity for self-improvement. Certainly, frustration with our current plight is a strong signal that we feel capable of more – as well as a key ingredient for developing a growth mindset. Yet this is a long way from the self-defeating view that we're 'worthless', 'unlovable' or even 'evil'. We're none of these things, unless we allow such negative self-beliefs to win. Again, the fact you're reading this book suggests both a desire for change and a degree of self-belief in your ability to change, which is the right sort of self-acceptance.

'Some people fear that if they accept themselves they will be lazy, arrogant and self-complacent,' says Sweet. 'This is usually just fear' – an excuse for inaction based on our inner conviction that we're incapable of change.

And, given the poor impact this negative acceptance is likely to have on our self-esteem and well-being, it can hardly be labelled self-acceptance at all: more like self-defeat.

Take responsibility

A final paradox. We are the guardians of our own future. No one is coming to our rescue, so we must take responsibility for our actions. Yet many under-confident people already feel responsible for their plight – often assuming that their poor status is their fault (probably repeating a script from their early conditioning).

'Feeling overly responsible for everything, all the time, can weigh very heavily on an individual's shoulders,' writes Sweet. 'It can lead to deep feelings of guilt, shame and self-loathing.'

Yet taking responsibility is a long way from absorbing blame. In fact, it's the opposite, because self-blame usually involves the language of surrender: 'I'm a bad person', 'that's just the way I am', 'I can't help myself'. This is a lazy form of responsibility based on absolving ourselves from the need for action. It's also based on a fixed mindset, while a growth mindset acknowledges the current (potentially negative) position – and our own role in creating it – yet embraces both the need for change and the fact it's our responsibility to execute change.

> **What's Stopping You Being More Confident?** *Having a 'characteristic thinking style' can dominate your reactions, reinforcing negative self-beliefs. But these can be challenged using cognitive behavioural therapy techniques. Yet you must accept that change will be unsettling. And you must take responsibility for the changes required.*

4
THE JOURNEY

As we have seen, confidence is a tool on our journey towards self-actualization – hence the need for a growth mindset and hence the use of CBT principles to question our (perhaps fixed) assumptions regarding our capabilities.

Certainly, there are traits for confidence – attributes to be acquired or at least understood (see Part Two). But if you're looking for a 'eureka' moment – when your life will change forever – you may be waiting in vain. Worse, you could end up wasting time and money (and the invested emotion of hope) on quick-fix techniques – such as hypnotism or acupuncture – that can boost confidence temporarily. Indeed, they may provide the sense of euphoria you seek. Yet so can alcohol or cocaine, with the inevitable hangover that follows.

Techniques such as hypnotism instil no more than an imitation of someone else's personality traits. You're being asked to become a different person: someone no less foreign to the real you than the person you become when drunk. At the very least this change in behaviour is based on the power of suggestion. Of course, there are those that say this is helpful. And mirroring the strong behaviour seen in others can, indeed, be effective. Yet our inner beliefs haven't changed.

We remain an under-confident person as well as one now requiring a 'fix' or, at the very least, obedience to someone's (perhaps subliminal) instructions. So while the techniques can make us feel elated and energized – these are not genuine feelings. They're borrowed feelings that may collapse at the first major setback: potentially rendering us more isolated, more inward-looking and more under-confident.

As with all instant gratifications, they rely on a hormonal release that – eventually – exacts a price.

Reversing your thinking

With no quick-fix injection available, is the entire premise of this book therefore flawed? Are your expectations of confidence overblown? If you're looking for immediate salvation, I'm afraid the answer is yes. But if you're looking to fully understand confidence, as well as the mental traps that destroy it, then the answer is no. A comprehension of confidence, and its opposite, can – in time and with persistence – reverse our thinking. We can stop adding layer upon layer to our poor confidence and, instead, start peeling away those layers. We can generate a distance between our current self and the under-confident person – adrift in our insecurities – that we once were.

For whatever reason, the under-confident person's view is distorted. What's more, they're making judgements based on this distortion. This book aims to point this out, as well as help sketch a view of what the world looks like without such distortions. But the hard work – the real work – is yours. You have to question every assumption you've ever made. Dispute every 'truth'.

Your views, values – even your principles – may have been distorted by the 'reality' you have constructed as self-protection. Indeed, even self-hatred can be a comforting disposition to the under-confident – an insulating layer based on building a firewall around you. 'That's just me', 'I cannot change', 'I will always be this way': all statements of surrender – mental sick notes excusing you from participation.

Tear up the sick note

So now's the time to tear up the sick note. Of course, your early actions are likely to be clumsy and fumbling. But realizing you're travelling the wrong path – and recognizing that you must change direction – is a strong first move. It's also a difficult one and therefore needs reinforcing if your mental turnaround is not to be reversed. So here are my Top 10 Tips for reinforcing your new, more constructive and growth-focused trajectory (and while a frivolous title, nothing below is written with anything other than serious intent).

1. *It's on your shoulders*
You cannot outsource your confidence. No one is going to be confident on your behalf. And there's no white knight coming to your rescue or guardian angel with your best interests at heart. You're alone, and the responsibility for action lies with you.

No matter how you found yourself in such a place, it's upon *your* shoulders to get beyond it. Of course, this sounds obvious. But it's an obvious lesson I spent years learning. Every time I met a successful or more confident person I played my 'save me' script in which I surreptitiously – even unconsciously – pleaded for help: perhaps angling the conversation towards a job offer or some other opening.

My salvation, I considered, was not in my hands – in fact, was beyond my capabilities. It needed the intervention of a more confident person who may or may not like me, or want to help me or even know how to help me. I was directionless, indiscriminate and so lacking in self-belief that I'd unconsciously beg strangers for salvation.

2. *Forgive*
To gain confidence, you must let go of the one thing you cannot change: the past. And this means forgiving those you may feel

destroyed your confidence when you were at your most vulnerable. Blaming others for your current poor confidence is a trap because it outsources responsibility to the very people who are least likely to help you.

Indeed, expecting others to have an epiphany, realize their guilt and then dedicate themselves to making amends is a vain hope and a recipe for prolonged frustration, anger and even depression. Blame is a disabling trait for those seeking confidence, and one worth challenging. Forgiveness, meanwhile, is your strongest weapon in helping you look to the future. Your forgiveness must be sincere, however. It must be meant, unconditional, uncompromising and in full.

Certainly, I forgive my father: a man whose upbringing was far tougher than mine. Devoid of love and even suffering abandonment (at five!), he had poor emotional reasoning with respect to my own upbringing and, anyway, felt he was simply applying the accepted norms of his time. And I have my father to thank for my strong sense of enquiry, my love of history and my work ethic.

'No one owes you a living,' was his common refrain, although he should have added 'or anything else'.

Indeed, I started making progress in my life only once the full meaning of that maxim became clear.

As for my sister – she doesn't need forgiveness because she's done nothing wrong. She was a child, barely older than me – an innocent dragged along by events and taking her cues from the adults around her. She's also been fantastically tolerant of her noisy, whimsical and self-obsessed brother over the years.

But you must also do more than forgive. You must develop your compassion for all those that have reinforced your poor confidence. Every incidence – adding all those layers to your poor confidence – must be revisited and seen from *their* point of view. Worried by their impact on you, you may have failed to see the impact you've had on *them*. After all, they are flesh and blood like yourself – with the same frailties, no matter what you think or how well they hide them. You need to search out the very human motivations of everyone you deal with – even those that hurt you.

3. *Kill the regret*

Of course, there's a danger in revisiting the past: regret. Since reversing my thinking – and developing a growth mindset – I've also developed what I call 'the cringe'. This is when a past negative event involuntarily floods back into my memory. My eyes close, my face screws and I even audibly gasp or sigh. Oh no, did I really do that? And say that? Was I so awful, so embarrassing, so unaware of what an idiot I was making of myself? Clearly, yes.

But then again, no. I'm picking tiny incidents over a lifetime of interactions – most of which went well enough for my brain to find no reason to remember them. The rare negatives have burnt into my memory because they generated fear and emotion, while the more common positives have been forgotten as the daily interactions of a normal human being.

Regret is self-sabotage in the extreme. It tells you there are a million positive paths you could have taken that you missed, somehow taking the only wrong turning in the road at every junction. This is – of course – nonsense. Each life will involve countless good and bad decisions – and good and bad reactions – with the vast balance in your favour and therefore not regretted and barely remembered. Yet it's the life sentence of the under-confident person to focus only on their losing shots – on their poor decisions and reactions – that stack up over the years and paralyze our future.

Of course, killing regret isn't easy – with many self-help gurus meandering into mysticism or self-hypnosis in order to do so. Yet there are more practical routes: perhaps writing down your 10 biggest regrets or mistakes, describing why they make you feel so awful (maybe because your more adult evaluations can now gauge a better, but missed, response), and then writing the key lessons you can take from the incident. Of course, this won't kill the 'cringe', but it will reinforce the growth mindset.

4. *Focus on the present*

In his famous book *How to Stop Worrying and Start Living* (1948), Dale Carnegie's appeal is that we 'live in day-tight compartments' – in the here and now, recognizing that 'today is our most precious possession'. So while much of your focus on gaining confidence should be future-oriented (see Part Three), it's today that really matters because – according to Carnegie – 'every day is a new life to a wise man'.

The aim here is not to replace regret about the past with worry about the future. It's the immediate that matters, taking the next action effectively in the hope that it can be executed well and build your confidence, rather than executed poorly and further under-mine your (perhaps fragile) resolve.

But tools are needed to help in this endeavour, and a key one should be keeping a diary. Indeed, this is a crucial point, and something virtually every self-help guru or technique agrees upon – and especially CBT. Keep a daily journal that records your thoughts, feelings, emotions, wins, setbacks, joys, despairs, tri-umphs and disasters. It's great to mark your progress. It's also a highly effective tactic for improving your evaluations. And it's a healthy addiction.

Winston Churchill kept a journal in which every day was headed 'Action of the Day'. Beneath he wrote his thoughts on what the action was and how best to achieve it. He would then execute his action and record its progress. This was a daily process that, over time, built his effectiveness as an operator – turning the awkward and under-confident schoolboy into the twentieth century's greatest statesman.

Indeed, Churchill's diary-keeping gives lie to the image of diary-writing as the exclusive concern of the pubescent and anxious. Virtually all of history's most eminent and successful people wrote a diary that recorded not only their daily activities but also their future plans and current tactics. And while adult diary-keeping is often viewed as the vanity of the self-important, it's possible to reverse this and say that many people became important simply because they utilized one of the most effective tools available to them: a daily journal helping align their immediate thoughts and actions with their goals and aspirations (see Part Three).

5. Look to the future

Of course, while focusing on the present, Churchill had a plan for his future. He always had a sense of his own destiny and his actions each day were no more than the execution of that destiny. Yet it was the plan that made it inevitable: nothing else. When I look back on my poor confidence – especially in my academic and career pursuits – the one thing I see above all else is a man with no plan.

How can progress be made if you have no idea what progress looks like? Of course it can't. And while Part Three will deal with this in more detail, it's worth noting here its importance for both the growth mindset (having an idea of what you grow towards) and the development of your confidence.

Confidence in what? Confidence for its own sake is both pointless and impossible (the world is simply too complex). Confidence requires you to discriminate. To make choices. And that requires you to look towards your idealized future – and develop confidence in what that idealized future entails.

And this is far from contradicting the previous need to focus on the present. With your future plans formulated, you can – indeed – develop a laser-like focus on the present because you'll be able to more accurately evaluate whether your current judgements support your future needs.

6. Destroy those negative tapes

Everyone has tapes that play in their heads. These are the scripts that, for the under-confident, are usually negative – along the lines of 'you cannot do this', or 'you are an idiot and are about to be found out', or 'you are not liked'.

Of course, these tapes can change behaviour in ways that make such confirmation more likely, which makes turning them off both imperative and challenging.

Yet it is possible. You just need to examine the facts. As with the CBT example of the man waiting for his date, many people jump to conclusions – and even reactions to those conclusions – while having only the most fractional data to go on. The fact she had yet to arrive led his internal jukebox to find and start the 'I've been rejected (again)' tape. In fact, the tape was probably already loaded, cued up and on pause waiting for the moment – perhaps one minute past the agreed meeting time (or even one minute to) – to play out.

Worse than this – for many, and certainly for me, the tape would have remained on pause even if she'd arrived on time. During the entire date, I would have searched her statements and body language for signs of rejection and the chance to run the tape. Signs that, of course, I'd have found or, if nothing became apparent (she was perhaps too polite), I'd have invented or even forced upon her.

Indeed, this is a tape with a mind of its own. And the only way of preventing it playing is to destroy it, which only a look at the hard facts can do.

In this instance:

- This is a unique date – no previous incident will act as a benchmark unless you allow it
- She agreed to the date
- She turned up!

The facts are all positive at this point – so negatively speculating beyond them is ridiculous: what psychologists call 'catastrophizing' (extrapolating already irrational thoughts to generate conclusions far worse than the current circumstances). Yet in so many incidents where confidence is required, it's those speculative and self-harming tapes that dictate our behaviour.

7. *Develop your autonomy*

To this day, I spend my life trying to please a particular person. As a child it was my father. Then it became various bosses or girlfriends. Now it's my wife. Their praise is my currency and my entire behaviour can be geared towards winning their favour. I will conceive, plan and execute a project with their praise in mind, and will judge success purely on that basis – becoming sulky and depressed if I fail to win sufficient praise.

This is a classic symptom of the under-confident – constantly looking for confirmation to the point where such confirmation is the most significant driver. Why? Because our poor self-beliefs have stripped us of any other benchmark. For whatever reason, we have no judgement regarding what's good or otherwise and seek confirmation from those we think have strong judgement.

Of course, this is nuts! We're not only handing them power they may not want and certainly don't need, we're destroying our own autonomy: making us no more than a slave to their whims.

In fact, getting beyond this is easy, although maintaining our autonomy is more difficult. To remove ourselves from their grip we simply need a credible plan for our future (see Part Three). You can then become a slave to *your* plan, rather than *their* praise. If your actions support your plan, then no further approval is required – making their praise a 'nice-to-have' rather than an imperative for your actions.

8. *Accept that you are work-in-progress*

You will remain work-in-progress for the rest of your life. There's no final destination. Even self-actualization generates new levels of need such as self-transcendence (i.e. focusing on others). Of course, this can be frustrating, although it shouldn't be. In fact, it's fantastically liberating. If you're free of the need for perfection then you're also free to act. You can try – fail – learn – try again. In fact, even if you don't fail you can try again – always taking your skills and endeavours to the next level.

Certainly, we need direction. But we've already established that fact and it'll come once we have the impetus to act. Deciding to act is the key, the direction comes next, and the notion of sustainable progress comes after that. It's a positive trajectory with the mechanism for failure built in as an alert for further learning and as a means for improvement.

9. *Sharpen the saw*

This is one of Stephen Covey's habits in his seminal work *Seven Habits of Highly Effective People* (1989). He draws on a parable of a woodman struggling to fell a tree with a blunt saw. 'Why don't you sharpen it?' an observer asks, only to be told: 'I haven't the time.'

Too often the under-confident person replaces inaction with over-action – what Stephen Covey calls 'busyness'. Enthused by the need to act, they throw themselves into emotion-fuelled endeavour – often with instruments (i.e. skills) too blunt or ill-suited for the job. So while it's essential to act, if we're not to encourage an immediate setback (at the very moment we're least prepared to endure it) we need to direct our energy towards 'sharpening the saw': i.e. acquiring the skills and tools we need for the journey.

Of course, in reality this is an alternative way of underlining the importance of planning and training. But it also dampens our passion. So often I read that we should 'follow our passions' in our pursuits. Yet passion is an emotional fuel that will dissipate once the going gets tough. Sure, choose a route based on your desires (see Part Three), but asking passion to sustain you on a long and uncertain journey will leave you exhausted, burnt-out and even embittered (hardly a recipe for improving your confidence). Only the momentum gained from small self-confirming steps towards a well-planned objective can turn the sprinter into a marathon runner – and one that builds confidence rather than spends passion.

10. *Fake it 'til you make it*

This sounds contradictory to the earlier advice of accepting you're work-in-progress. How can you accept that you're work-in-progress while masquerading as the finished article? Indeed, how can you be true to yourself while lying to the world?

You cannot – but that's not what this is saying. The message here is that you cannot move towards confidence and retain the outward persona of an under-confident person. Modesty, self-deprecation – even demureness – are defensive traits based on deflecting scrutiny and hiding poor confidence. And they need to be swapped for something more effective.

Of course, becoming pompous or bumptious or self-aggrandizing will be equally harmful – not least because these are borrowed traits that will quickly be revealed as such. But to face forward while making no adjustment in the way you conduct or project yourself is asking for those you meet to confirm your previously under-confident state, rather than to acknowledge the changes underway.

Take the example of our treatment in a shop or restaurant: if we continue to behave as if we expect poor service – as if we assume they've spotted our low status and are taking their cues from this observation – we cannot be surprised if that's, indeed, how they treat us. Yet if we 'fake it' – meaning that we conjure strong confidence (consciously prior to entering if necessary) – we are communicating our expectation of good service, which is likely to have an impact on *their* behaviour.

Humans shouldn't be so triggered by such shallow affectations – I agree. But we are, so we need to be aware of this and act accordingly. At first this may feel awkward or foreign. Yet observing the difference in reactions should encourage us – with each small victory adding further confirmation that we're heading in the right direction.

In fact, such affectations are easy (and, I now realize, also adopted by the confident). They include:

- *Smile*. This usually encourages a smile in return. Likewise, frowns encourage frowns.
- *Be smart*. Dress like you're there to fix the toilet and that's how you'll be treated. Dress well, and you're immediately communicating your expectation of being treated well.

- *Walk tall.* Stand upright, walk confidently, enter boldly and speak clearly. '*Good morning!*' – said with enough authority that their return of the compliment is almost an involuntary reflex.
- *Assume you're welcome.* Again, they're likely to mimic your assumption and, indeed, make you welcome.

Too nerve-wracking? OK, why not pursue my previous tactic of avoiding any shop or restaurant in which poor treatment was even a possibility? You'll not be challenged but – over time – your world will close down: rendering you confused, bitter and less confident than ever. Far better to adopt a growth mindset and experiment with the idea you can take responsibility for your actions, and even help encourage better reactions in others.

> **What's Stopping You Being More Confident?** *You must tear up the sick note and participate. To do this you must move on from the past (including forgiving those you think may have harmed you) – and you must develop autonomy by focusing on the future and accepting that you remain work-in-progress.*

PART TWO
The Alchemy of Confidence

5
OPTIMISM AND RESILIENCE

Confidence isn't simply the absence of under-confidence. It's an alchemy of positive traits that, when mixed, create something greater than the sum of its parts. To develop confidence, therefore, we must understand what's in that mix. I mean fully understand – calculating what *must* be acquired, as well as what we simply need to comprehend and even what we can potentially dismiss as little more than a myth.

Certainly, there are some powerful illusions in the confidence mix. But there are also traits that cannot be ignored – probably the most important of which is optimism. Confident people not only hope for the best, they assume it. And it's this – above all else – that allows them to act.

For me, pessimism (optimism's opposite) feels like an innate condition – an albatross around my neck that's been there my entire life. Of course, this isn't true. I became a pessimist from negative early-life experiences. Nonetheless, pessimism acts as a powerful brake on my endeavours – inwardly convincing me that even 'normal' is probably unsustainable and that anything better than normal is almost certainly setting me up for a terrible reckoning.

And like much else, my pessimism is self-fulfilling. I create the conditions that endorse my negative outlook – even seeking out the news that confirms it. Constantly standing on my metaphorical bridge scouring the horizon for icebergs, I can change course or even jump ship at the merest white speck on the horizon, which – of course – adds yet another layer to my poor confidence.

Given such a disabling prospect – and one that seems so ingrained – can optimism ever be learnt? According to University of Pennsylvania psychologist Martin E.P. Seligman it can. In his groundbreaking 1990 book *Learned Optimism,* Seligman sets out to explore the notion of optimism by defining it in terms of how we inwardly explain successes and failures: what he calls our 'explanatory style'.

For Seligman, my search for icebergs is part of my pessimistic explanatory style, although it's a classic characteristic of an under-confident person. Yet both pessimistic and optimistic styles are a choice, he says, because – even with pessimism – we're generating a belief in our own inabilities that has little to do with reality (at least initially): what Seligman calls 'learned helplessness'.

Pessimists view setbacks as 'perpetual, pervasive and personal', says Seligman. They are a reflection and confirmation of the pessimist's poor self-beliefs and are, therefore, viewed as final. Meanwhile, optimists explain setbacks as no more than unwanted interruptions.

'Look for the link between your beliefs and the consequences,' says Seligman. 'Pessimistic explanations set out passivity and dejection whereas optimistic explanations energize.'

The link with control

Pessimism derives from a deep-seated sense that events are beyond our control and therefore probably, if not inevitably, negative. Again, optimists believe the opposite: that things are, mostly, within their control and that those that aren't are of no consequence, or – at least – not worth brooding upon.

But, Seligman insists, optimism *can* be learnt. A central problem for pessimists, he says, is our (by now familiar) poor conditioning, brought about by negative past events: each piling up on the other to create an unchallenged narrative of learned helplessness. Yet if we challenge such negative evaluations (as with the CBT examples in Part One) we can 'inoculate' ourselves against helplessness – turning our pessimism/optimism dial in the right direction. Optimism in this respect is simply the challenging of those pessimistic narratives – the 'unlearning' of unconscious and automatic negative reactions by consciously going on the offensive.

'By effectively disputing the beliefs that follow adversity, you can change your customary reaction from dejection and giving up to activity and good cheer,' claims Seligman.

Optimistic explanations

Optimism generates resilience (see below), and resilience (or otherwise) comes down to the explanations people give themselves when things go wrong. Explanations that, if unhelpful, we can actively reverse, says Seligman.

His tips for doing this include the following (with some thoughts of my own):

1. *Reversing your view of temporary and permanent factors.* Pessimists view positive events as temporary – even illusionary – and negative events as a resumption of 'normal service': hence my search for the 'inevitable' (though metaphorical) icebergs. Optimists do the opposite. An optimistic lottery winner explains that 'I'm always lucky' while the pessimist will see it as 'my lucky day', and may even worry about the price to be paid for such luck. Assuming some mystical rebalancing is inevitable is obvious nonsense, however – no more than superstition. It's also an assumption we *must* challenge.

2. *Challenging the pervasiveness of negative events.* Pessimists assume negativity runs right across the various aspects of their life. Meanwhile, optimists can isolate negativity, seeing it as a

'tricky situation' in a single area while other zones remain unaffected. With thought (and the use of our diary to help separate the zones), this can be achieved by the pessimist.

3. *Depersonalization.* The pessimist's 'explanatory style' will involve internalizing the blame for a negative event. Yet constantly blaming ourselves when things go wrong can lead to low self-esteem and even depression (see Part Five), while externalizing the blame prevents damage to our self-esteem and supports our optimistic view of the world (and certainly ourselves). While we need to take responsibility for our actions, we shouldn't automatically assume the blame every time something negative occurs and we certainly shouldn't absorb it as 'typical' or 'deserved'. It's just an event or a run of unconnected events – so connecting it with our personality is a ridiculous own goal.

4. *Killing rumination.* 'Failure makes everyone at least momentarily helpless,' says Seligman, 'but the hurt goes away – for some people almost instantly. . . . For others, the hurt lasts; it seethes, it rolls, it congeals into a grudge.'

   Seligman's view is that ruminating on past failures is more a female than male trait (although one I'm guilty of, for sure). Women tend to be more self-analytical, he states, while men are better at resisting dwelling on mistakes – perhaps by distracting themselves in a way that breaks the negative cycle. In this instance, therefore, it's typically-male behaviour that should be emulated, as Seligman warns that unchallenged rumination can lead to depression, and is certainly a recipe for pessimism.

5. *Breaking the cycle.* People who accumulate bad life events tend to become worn down, says Seligman. They can even end up generating pessimistic responses to positive events (such as the 'price' of a lottery win, as discussed earlier), which – of course – means that pessimists will inevitably experience more negative events (making pessimism, like poor confidence, self-fulfilling). Over time, many pessimists become passive and isolate themselves, or they adopt unhealthy lifestyles that make

negative events almost inevitable. Yet changing this can be as simple as joining a gym or starting a sport, or turning some physical or mental activity into a habit that helps reverse the trajectory of deterioration.

Countering learned helplessness

The easiest way for a pessimist to reverse the spiral of 'learned helplessness', however, is to adopt what Seligman calls 'flexible optimism'. This is an approach well short of blind optimism, which Seligman also sees as an unhealthy state. 'Flexible optimism' is simply expanding our pessimism–optimism spectrum, so that we consider optimistic outcomes possible, and also consider the potential limits of our pessimism.

For instance, if we obsess about the potential downside of an action, it requires us to consider boundaries to the fallout (avoiding catastrophic assumptions), as well as impose additional questions on ourselves such as 'what's the alternative view?'.

A crucial benefit of 'flexible optimism' is that it reinforces rather than undermines the strongest card of the pessimist, which is realism. The pessimist doesn't have to ignore his or her own – perhaps evidence-based – view of reality. We simply have to ensure that such a view is balanced: considering both the limits of the pessimistic point-of-view and at least the potential for an optimistic upside.

Resilience – more than coping

Importantly, flexible optimism prevents us becoming fantasists – meaning we don't have to ignore the fact that, in certain circumstances, things indeed are bad. And it can help us deal with the unexpected, which has an important influence on another key requirement for confidence: resilience.

'Resilience implies more than just coping,' writes Charlotte Style in *Brilliant Positive Psychology* (2011). 'Resilience grows from *healthy* coping.'

Again, this is an area where I constantly fall down. I seem incapable of absorbing knocks and setbacks without them deeply impacting my self-esteem. Buoyed by happy events – such as winning a new client – I can immediately find myself in a state of mental collapse from the smallest piece of bad news, or even the prospect that bad news is on the horizon. Of course, this is the opposite to resilience, which is being irrepressible – absorbing the punches without any impact on our overall outlook or conviction.

Like so much else, resilience is developed in childhood: often learnt, or otherwise, vicariously from a parent who may themselves have had strong or poor coping skills. Yet resilience is often misunderstood. It isn't about survival, which may have been achieved at enormous emotional cost or trauma – perhaps damaging our confidence or even generating post-traumatic stress disorder. It's about coming through stressful or negative situations with *more* confidence, not less.

That said, care is required. As with optimism, resilience still requires realism.

'This is not an invitation to become delusional!' exclaims Style.

Rose-tinted views may pull us through but may be denying an essential truth. Resilience is more about being constructive: seeking the positive, expanding upon it, and focusing on how we can prosper from the current reality no matter what the negatives.

'As with all things,' says Style, 'the trick is to mitigate the thinking that spirals us downwards and to reinforce the thinking that spirals us upwards. We just need to turn the knob appropriately.'

Resilience under stress

Timing adds a further dimension to resilience. Being resilient eventually doesn't count. We must be able to draw on our fortitude at the very moment our confidence is challenged. Of course, these moments may take us by surprise – arriving at the instant we're least prepared. Yet that's the point with resilience. We need to show resilience under pressure. We must cope with stressful situations as they occur – not after we've calmed down following an emotional collapse.

'The reality is that most people fail in extreme situations,' says writer Paul Sullivan in his popular book *Clutch: Why Some People Excel Under Pressure and Others Don't* (2010). 'When the pressure mounts, their ability leaves them. They choke.'

By '*clutch*' Sullivan is referring to American sporting slang for an ability to perform well under extreme pressure – or 'in the clutch' (i.e. at the key moment). 'Transferring what you can do in a relaxed atmosphere to a tenser one is not easy,' says Sullivan, 'or else everyone would be in the *clutch*.'

Clutch can be learnt

Sullivan claims that the ability to cope under pressure can be learnt, as long as we can first deal with the emotional aspects of stressful situations. For Sullivan, the following attributes are vital:

1. *Focus.* 'Most people confuse focus with concentration,' says Sullivan. Yet Sullivan's *clutch* requires a laser-like focus on the crisis or concern at hand, making our assessment of the whole situation important. Concentration, meanwhile, may mean becoming obsessed on a single aspect – perhaps as a defence mechanism to prevent the whole overwhelming us. Sullivan cites top trial lawyers (barristers in the UK) who remain focused on every aspect of a court case – skipping instantly and effectively between them as the tension mounts.

2. *Discipline.* Making decisions under pressure requires a clear head and an ability to remove unhelpful criteria. Undisciplined individuals load their decision-making with emotional and

intellectual baggage, says Sullivan. Certainly, people become less rational when stressed, meaning they make instinctive decisions perhaps based on their fears.

3. *Adapting.* Stressful situations are the very moments well-planned strategies usually disintegrate. Yet a focus on our objectives (see Part Three) should give us strong judgement – aiding adaptability despite the heat of battle. According to Sullivan, it's inflexibility at these critical points that most often results in the snapping of our brittle resolve.

4. *'Being present.'* In a battle, 'now' is all that matters. 'Embrace the present,' says Sullivan, citing actors on stage who have to adopt an emotion or act a character instantly. If their mind wanders beyond that moment they're likely to falter, says Sullivan. For me, however, this is less impressive than watching a TV news-anchor switch focus to a new subject the instant after a combative interview with a political heavyweight.

Choking

The opposite to Sullivan's *clutch* is choking: i.e. collapsing under pressure. Choking derives from not taking responsibility for your actions, says Sullivan, as well as from overthinking. The fear of 'owning your failure' makes you prioritize excuses rather than actions (wrecking focus, discipline and adaptability), while over-thinking destroys clarity and fluidity of thought and makes you doubt your decision-making.

Obviously, sport provides choking's most famous examples – with few more so than the 1993 Wimbledon final between Jana Novotna and Steffi Graf. In fact, this incident is so famous, Malcolm Gladwell uses it as his key case study when writing about the subject in his 2009 book, *What The Dog Saw*.

'There was a moment in the third and deciding set . . . when Jana Novotna seemed invincible,' he wrote. 'She was leading 4–1 and serving at 40–30, meaning that she was one point from winning the game, and just five points from the most coveted championship in tennis . . . and then something happened. She served the ball straight into the net. She stopped and steadied herself for the second serve . . . but this time it was worse. . . . Double fault. At game point, she hit an overhead straight into the net. Instead of 5–1, it was now 4–2. Graf to serve: an easy victory, 4–3. Novotna to serve. She wasn't tossing the ball high enough. Her head was down. Her movements had slowed markedly . . . 4–4. Did she suddenly realize how terrifyingly close she was to victory? Did she remember that she had never won a major tournament before? Did she look across the net and see Steffi Graf – Steffi Graf! – the greatest player of her generation?'

Of course, Graf went on to win, resulting in that celebrated cameo of Novotna sobbing on the Duchess of Kent's shoulder.

Preventing choking

So what steps can overcome choking – helping us develop an ability to perform in critical and stressful situations? Sullivan suggests the following:

- *Accept.* Avoid denying that the situation is upon you. Neither hope nor denial will make it go away. You are where you are, so deal with it.
- *Readjust.* Anger, self-pity, regret – all will prevent you seeing reality and may lead to surrender. Coldly and clinically assess your situation: the positives as well as the negatives. Work out what's possible, given current circumstances, and what isn't.
- *Prioritize.* Another key need is to work out what decisions and choices have to be made, when, and make them. If you're under pressure you must *own the change*, not have it thrust upon you.
- *Take responsibility.* Now is not the time to apportion blame as it will disable your thinking. By taking responsibility,

meanwhile, you're also taking charge of the resolution, which is highly enabling.

- *Focus on outcomes.* Looking forward rather than back is vital, so it's therefore also important to know what 'looking forward' looks like. By quickly determining what the outcome should be – and by focusing on that outcome – you can acquire the judgement and adaptability resilience requires.

The heat of the battle

Of course, much of the above is easy to say but harder to achieve, especially in the heat of battle when our emotions are triggered and our hormones are pumping. In such circumstances we can be everything we shouldn't: denying our current status, focusing on regret rather than outcomes, reactively blaming others (and seeking results that highlight their guilt).

Yet we shouldn't be so hard on ourselves. As long as they don't disable us, emotions are better out than in. And they may also be needed for absorbing the new reality: they're a genuine reaction, after all, and a step towards Sullivan's need for acceptance. In this respect, an emotional response that acts as an alert, and that quickly alters our attitudes towards the new – urgent – reality, may be healthier for our resilience (and therefore our confidence) than denial, even if such a front gives an initial outward impression of both resilience and confidence.

And like many of the traits for confidence, resilience isn't built overnight. It's a construction that takes time to develop. After all, Novotna went on to win Wimbledon five years later.

> **What's Stopping You Being More Confident?** *Poor conditioning generates pessimism, which is 'learned helplessness'. 'Learned optimism' is simply the challenging and limiting of these negative explanations. Resilience, meanwhile, requires focus, discipline and flexibility.*

6

SELF-EFFICACY AND TALENT

It's a description that crops up again and again in self-help books – apparently outlining the critical difference between those with and without confidence. So what is 'self-efficacy' (pronounced 'ef-i-kuh-see')? And why is it so important for developing confidence in previously under-confident people?

The dictionary definition declares efficacy as the 'capacity for producing the desired end result'. Therefore, *self*-efficacy – according to Daniel Goleman in his seminal work *Emotional Intelligence* (1996) – is no more than 'the [self-] belief that one has mastery over the events of one's life and can meet challenges as they come up'.

This makes self-efficacy more than the dictionary's 'capacity': it's competence with added self-belief. It's the self-knowledge that we have strong skills in a particular area, as well as the fact we – indeed – possess such skills. Our beliefs are not illusionary.

Of course, developing competence in a particular area should strengthen our self-efficacy. And this should increase our willingness to take greater risks – to push the boundaries of our talents or acquired skills, making us willing to develop new skills in tangentially-relevant areas. All of which will add to our confidence.

'People's beliefs about their abilities have a profound effect on those abilities,' writes Stanford psychologist and leading authority of self-efficacy Albert Bandura in *Self-efficacy: The Exercise of Control* (1997). 'Ability is not a fixed property; there is a huge variability in how to perform.'

Belief in our skills

Study after study has shown, says Bandura, that – when tested at the start of a programme for work or education – it's those with higher levels of self-efficacy that perform better than those with a higher IQ or stronger levels of professional training or attainment. Skill alone is not enough. We have to believe in our skills.

Certainly, people will be more inclined to take on a task if they believe they can succeed, and will be more inclined to avoid tasks if they fear failure. This much may be obvious, but – we must remember – self-efficacy's link with actual competence is via self-belief. The two halves of self-efficacy (competence and belief) must be in balance. Over-estimating our abilities could mean we attempt tasks beyond our skills with potentially disastrous results (not least for our confidence). Optimum self-efficacy, therefore, is ahead of our *current* abilities, but not ahead of our *potential* capabilities, which – of course – we may still be discovering.

Self-efficacy is self-reinforcing

While self-efficacy is therefore part belief and part actual competence, it's wholly self-reinforcing – as is its opposite.

'The thought 'I can't do this' is crippling,' says Goleman, who lists symptoms of poor self-efficacy as:

- Being paralyzed by the fear of public humiliation (fear of failure)
- Failing to voice potentially valuable ideas
- Readily giving up our opinions and judgements, or dismissing even strongly held ideas at the first (even mild) challenge
- Chronic indecision – especially under pressure
- Shying away from even the smallest risk.

Low self-efficacy can therefore lead people into believing a task is harder than it actually is. There are also wild differences in task execution observed by those with high and low self-efficacy. Those with low self-efficacy approach tasks erratically – perhaps plunging in unpredictably before changing direction many times. Meanwhile, those with high self-efficacy tend to hold back – taking a wider view of the task before making more accurate and effective moves.

Another difference is in overcoming obstacles. Those with high self-efficacy can even be encouraged by barriers, seeing them as a test of their approach – perhaps requiring a greater effort or refinement. Those with low self-efficacy, however, see obstacles as the trigger for a change in direction or even as the moment to surrender the task as 'undoable'. And if the task does result in failure, those with high self-efficacy will likely attribute their failure to factors such as being below par that day or poor preparation. Predictably, those with low self-efficacy will blame their innate inabilities.

Roots of self-efficacy

The self-help gurus are therefore right. Self-efficacy is a major requirement for confidence. Yet – like optimism – it's something that can be learned, although we first need to understand how we arrived at our current level of self-efficacy. Bandura outlines four potential sources:

1. *Experience.* Most obviously, if we succeed at something, our self-efficacy levels increase. If we fail, they are lowered. Children that succeed develop the confidence to keep going. Meanwhile, those that fail are disheartened.
2. *Modelling.* We're constantly comparing ourselves to others. When we see someone else succeed, we also see their self-efficacy increase and we mimic their behaviour in order to also gain from the experience. Indeed, witnessing a similarly-adept person succeed is often enough to increase our own

self-efficacy – not least because the example increases our desire, and therefore determination, to also master the task. Yet it's not difficult to imagine our despair when our modelling fails.

3. *Social persuasions.* Were we encouraged or discouraged when children? Most people can remember times when parents or peers played a strong influence on their self-efficacy. For instance, I can remember my father saying I'd one day make an excellent driver. I passed my driving test first time and for years assumed myself more than competent behind the wheel. In fact, I'm no more than an average driver. Yet that one state-ment made an enormous difference to my early self-efficacy behind the wheel.

4. *Physiological factors.* Stressful situations can induce physical reactions that we misinterpret as low self-efficacy. An example of my own involves speaking engagements, which always make me nervous. The adrenaline flows and I sweat profusely, yet I used to interpret this as a sign of poor competence when speaking (regarding both delivery and content). Now more experienced at speaking – and more confident with my content – I realize the physiological reactions can equally be interpreted as excited anticipation.

Self-efficacy is domain-specific

Yet self-efficacy has its limits, not least the fact it's 'domain-specific' according to Bandura. This means we can gain strong self-efficacy in one area that has no impact on our confidence elsewhere. Being at the top of our profession, for instance, makes us no better at playing golf – hence those famous dilemmas when on the course with the boss.

Nonetheless, gaining self-efficacy in one area is beneficial if we can recognize what's happened and apply the methodology to gain self-efficacy elsewhere. It won't be automatic. The same level of endeavour is required. Yet we have the knowledge of gaining strong competence in something – largely because we believed ourselves capable of such advancement and worked hard to achieve it – so surely we can expand our range of talents?

The myth of talent

And it's here that self-efficacy overlaps with talent. Certainly, talent is a seemingly obvious trait for confidence: except that talent is a myth. At least that's the view of a range of writers on the subject, including Geoff Colvin (*Talent is Overrated: What Really Separates World-Class Performers from Everybody Else*, 2008), Daniel Coyle (*The Talent Code: Greatness isn't Born. It's Grown*, 2010), Matthew Syed (*Bounce: The Myth of Talent and the Power of Practice*, 2011), John C. Maxwell (*Talent is Never Enough*, 2007) and Malcolm Gladwell (*Outliers: The Story of Success*, 2008).

The titles say it all. High achievers are no more talented than many others, say researchers. Yet they're more focused, more committed and – above all – extremely hard working: prepared to repeat perhaps mundane tasks again and again in their drive for perfection.

Mozart, Tiger Woods, Warren Buffett – all very capable children, says Colvin in *Talent is Overrated*, but all worked prodigiously hard to raise themselves above the herd. For instance, according to Colvin, research into musical students found no link between their precociousness and their subsequent high performance. Instead, the link was found with the number of hours they practised.

'The difference between expert performers and normal adults reflects a life-long period of deliberate effort to improve performance in a specific domain,' says Colvin, citing violinists that became 'the best' through practising by themselves around 24 hours a week, while the 'good' violinists, managed just nine.

By 18, the best violin students will have accumulated thousands more hours of practice than their peers, says Colvin: perhaps a total of around 7000 hours compared to 5000 or so for those that are merely 'good' and 3400 for 'third-level' musicians. And that creates a powerful link with confidence, which requires a laser-like focus on learning the attributes of a required skill and the dedication to repeat the task until it becomes second nature. There are no short cuts. No alternative routes. Colvin states that we need to practice again and again – perhaps breaking the skill into elements – until we not only get it right but can repeat that level of performance on demand.

IQ has little bearing

As it is for skills such as music, so it is for knowledge. Of course, the IQs of those that excel are sometimes brilliant, but just as often they're no more than average and in many cases below average. Certainly, IQ has little bearing on our standing within a particular field, which will have been attained through years of endeavour. In fact, Colvin claims that the reverse can be true. While IQ has little or no bearing on performance, dedicating the time and effort required to memorize relevant material can have a beneficial impact on our cognitive (i.e. mental) abilities.

Colvin cites chess champions who, over time, learn to predict moves that the average player cannot perceive, and the singer whose range can be expanded by training – both suggesting that (as with Dweck's growth mindset) there's no point at which they consider themselves 'full' with respect to their expertise.

'Great performers never allow themselves to reach the automatic, arrest-development state in their chosen field,' says Colvin. 'That is the effect of continual deliberate practice – avoiding automaticity.'

And Colvin points to another attribute of the high-performer – one that works in favour of the under-confident person. Talented people are incredibly hard on themselves. No matter what, their discontent remains. They think they can, and should, be achieving more. Many feel like imposters in their chosen field, despite laudable and externally-recognised attainment. And it's this feeling that often drives them on – forcing them to practice harder and harder in order to get better and better.

Of course, the above offers no immediate confidence, and potentially says that full confidence can never be gained, no matter how competent we become. Yet – as we have seen – confidence in its widest sense is a myth, or at best a blind alley, potentially leading us towards hubris and calamity (see Part Five). True confidence – i.e. self-efficacy – is an awareness of our current capabilities and a belief in our capacity for improvement. This is a journey: and one reinforced by the concept that talent is something we work at, not something we innately possess.

The Mozart exception?

A last myth-buster with respect to talent involves age and genius. Starting young offers obvious advantages, but why do prodigies exist in music and maths, asks Colvin, but not in literature and physics? He offers the answer that children become prodigies in areas where they can be pushed. Tiger Woods was introduced to golf at the age of two by his father, Earl, a golf enthusiast. Meanwhile, tennis champions Serena and Venus Williams can, again, thank their father (Richard) for their tennis careers. Lewis Hamilton, too, needs to say a big 'cheers, dad' to his father, Anthony, for his Formula 1 racing career.

Sure, all were 'talented' in that they were capable of learning and strong enough to cope with the intensity of training. But all owe their success to a wilful and ambitious parent who got them started when they were toddlers – not to some magic dust sprinkled upon them at birth.

But what about Mozart, most ask at this point: composing works for the violin at five, playing to audiences at six, producing professionally-acclaimed work by 10?

'Surely here is an example of a man who was born with his sublime abilities intact,' writes Matthew Syed in *Bounce*. 'A man who came to the world stamped with the mark of genius.'

Syed then goes on to explore Mozart's relationship with his father Leopold. A renowned composer in his own right, the older Mozart was best known among his contemporaries for authoring the leading work on childhood violin instruction. Domineering and persistent, Leopold started his son on an intensive programme of training and composition from the age of three. And it may also be worth noting that Mozart's first work to universally herald his 'genius' – the Piano Concerto No. 9 – was written when he was 21 (after no less than 18 years of instruction).

Experience counts

One final observation from Colvin worth noting is that, with all these prodigies, we see a life focused on teachable talents in music or sport or other learnable and technical endeavours such as maths. Yet in many fields, real expertise comes from wisdom. And that requires experience.

There are few (genuine – i.e. not 'shock') prodigies in the arts and none in the professions (including the sciences and law) or academia. Youthful entrepreneurs tend to rise and fall with equal rapidity, as do businessmen and politicians promoted too soon (though many rise again). In these walks of life, experiences are valued as highly as talent because experience gives the practitioner wisdom, and wisdom is a key attribute for confidence as well as something that no pushy parent or star-spotting coach can provide to a youngster.

And this is good news for the under-confident adult looking to gain confidence as a deliberate pursuit. Sure, if taking up tennis in our 30s or golf in our 40s, we may have left it too late for a career as a Grand Slam champion, but there are plenty of areas in which we can excel – as long as we're prepared to make the commitment and put in the hours.

What's Stopping You Being More Confident? *Self-efficacy is belief and competence combined, and is a key attribute of the confident, making its acquisition worth the effort. Yet it remains domain-specific, as does talent – which is nearly always a result of endeavour.*

7

COURAGE AND EXTRAVERSION

Mettle, nerve, guts, grit, chutzpah, daring, spunk: however you want to label it, courage is something that the confident seem to possess in spades and the under-confident seem to lack. In fact, it can seem like their defining quality – allowing confident people to advance while the under-confident hesitate, and therefore languish in frustration and feelings of inadequacy.

Yet courage is a confusing concept. For instance, many people think I'm brave because I've the courage to do things (such as write books on my insecurities). Others, meanwhile, see this as merely foolish – action without strategy that could be harmful to my long-term well-being. So how can we discern courage, which is a noble quality that supports our confidence, from daft recklessness, which will ultimately undermine it?

'Courage is a deep-seated fundamental competence that leverages our other abilities,' writes Gus Lee in *Courage*, his 2006 book on what he calls the *backbone of leadership*. 'It invokes within us our best selves.'

This makes courage an additional layer to self-efficacy: it's competence and belief coated with an ability to act, which is about as far from foolish bravado as it's possible to get. Yet, at least externally, they look the same, making differentiation a key need. In fact, that's the point – if the difference is not obvious internally (i.e. in our own minds), it must be foolishness (because the competence is clearly missing). Of course, this is nothing to beat ourselves up about – it just means we have work to do.

'[Courage] is not a gift bestowed by Providence on only a few rarely endowed individuals,' writes Dale Carnegie in *How to Develop Self-Confidence and Influence People by Public Speaking* (1957), the book of his series that pays most attention to courage. 'It is like the ability to play golf. Anyone can develop his own latent capacity if he has sufficient desire to do so.'

And while Carnegie was addressing public speaking (and possibly golf!), he hits upon a key concept for developing courage: practice. By increasing our competence, preparation and practice will remove the terror, says Carnegie, giving us the courage – despite our insecurities or fears – to act. And while this seems like an overly-simple solution from an old-fashioned writer, it's also true. As I've indeed learnt with public speaking, it's a lot less terrifying with good preparation and some practice before each event. That said, such was my terror before my first speech, I nearly failed to show up.

Acting despite our fears

Crucially, by this definition (of gaining courage through competence) we're not removing fear. We're simply giving ourselves the ability to act *despite* our fears, something Susan Jeffers broaches in her totemic work *Feel the Fear and Do it Anyway* (1987).

'We can't escape fear,' she writes. 'We can only transform it into a companion that accompanies us in all our existing adventures; it is not an anchor holding us transfixed in one spot'. In other words, if we aim to make progress, fear – to a lesser or greater degree – is a near-certain companion.

Jeffers cites five 'truths about fear' (with some thoughts of my own):

1. *As long as we continue to grow, fear will never go away.* This takes us back to Carol Dweck's growth mindset, and the fact the only way to eliminate fear is to stop growing, although – in my opinion – the fear will chase us even then: forcing us to live in ever-decreasing circles. If fear is therefore inevitable, we may as well push forward, which means the fear we encounter will at least be the positive fear of progress.

2. *The only way to get rid of the fear of doing something is to do it.* This seems an obvious point, although many under-confident people ignore this patent truth through avoidance.

3. *'Doing it' makes us feel better while avoiding it makes us feel worse.* Sure, doing it and falling flat on our face isn't great, but we can treat failure as a positive learning experience (as long as we are prepared to learn the lesson and try again). Yet walking away from a challenge because we lack the courage is a sure-fire way of destroying our confidence and reinforcing feelings of low self-esteem.

4. *Everyone feels fear when they are in unfamiliar territory.* Of course, others may be more effective at hiding it – developing potentially sophisticated masks. Nonetheless, some fear of the unknown is a given (and sensible): it's whether our fear prevents us taking action that divides us.

5. *Pushing through fear is less frightening than living with the fear of helplessness.* As the title of Jeffers' book states, the point is not to avoid fear but to stop fear arresting our endeavours – and that takes courage.

Developing courage – perseverance

Inevitably, psychologists offer a more technical take on fear. Writing in *The Oxford Companion to the Mind* (edited by Richard L. Gregory, 1987), eminent British psychologist Stanley Rachman combines fear and courage under the same heading – reinforcing the link. Yet he denotes a major division between *acute* fears, which are provoked by a 'tangible stimulus' that subsides quickly once that stimulus is removed (a fear of snakes being an example), and *chronic* fears, which are intangible and therefore more complex. Fear of aging or being alone, or fear of failure, are examples of chronic fears – all of which can produce long-term alterations in behaviour based on the desire to avoid those fears being triggered.

According to Rachman, courage is defined as 'the occurrence of perseverance despite fear', which concurs with Jeffers imploring us to 'do it anyway' as well as with Lee's views regarding leveraging our competences. Certainly, training for courage helps professionals such as soldiers and fire-fighters undertake dangerous jobs, with the introduction to danger graduated through a process psychologists call 'desensitization': the step-by-step deconstruction of our fears into elements that are then dealt with through training and practice (not dissimilar to CBT's 'exposure technique').

Developing courage – motivation

As well as desensitization to fear, Rachman points to one other 'courage training' need – motivation or 'desire', to use the more emotive word in Carnegie's quote. If we desire something enough we can, surely, develop the courage to act in order to acquire it.

That said, we should beware foolishness, which can be a side-effect of desire. Having long-term goals should help (see Part Three) because we become motivated, not by our desires, but by our plans for achieving them, which should also improve our judgement (see below) – helping us gauge the difference between courage and bravado.

What's not on offer, however, is fearlessness, despite Rachman – using parachutists as an example – considering such a state possible. Veteran jumpers, he feels, can reach fearlessness once they operate within their comfort zone and no longer 'push the boundaries'. But to make progress we have to accept fear as a constant companion, making courage a key need.

Extraversion – the incautious personality

Yet courage should not be confused with extraversion (also spelt extroversion) despite generating seemingly-similar external behaviours. In fact, extraversion is a personality type: one half of the extravert-introvert divide popularized by legendary psychologist Carl Jung (see 'What the psychologists say' at the back of the book).

The *extravert* has an outward flow of personal energy – making them sociable, enthusiastic and incautious, although also potentially shallow, unreflective and volatile. Meanwhile, the *introvert* is characterized by an inward flow of personal energy – making them imaginative, self-contained and reflective, although also potentially shy, hesitant and withdrawn.

Of course, for the under-confident this could be immediately revelatory. Are we simply introverts: a Jungian personality type based on ancient cultural inheritances, and a potentially positive realization after a lifetime thinking that we were socially inept or lacked confidence?

Certainly, introverts 'tend to be more reserved and less outspoken in large groups', writes Ros Taylor in *Confidence at Work* (2011). 'They often take pleasure in solitary activities such as reading, writing, drawing and using computers.'

Taylor points out that the archetypal artist, writer, sculptor or composer is usually introverted – making introversion a potentially-desirable quality.

'Introverts are likely to enjoy time spent alone and find less reward in time spent with large groups of people, though they tend to enjoy interactions with close friends,' says Taylor.

Yet, despite the obvious benefits of under-confident people reframing themselves as introverts, we're concerned here with confidence, which – at least externally – requires the attributes of the extravert. In many cases society still seems to consider introversion an affliction in need of a cure, which means being an introvert is unlikely to boost our confidence.

'Our culture values and rewards the qualities of extroverts,' says psychoanalyst Marti Olsen Laney in *The Introvert Advantage* (2002) – echoing Jung, who said, somewhat regretfully, that society favours the extravert.

Describing today's world as a rock concert rather than a museum trip, Olsen Laney considers that we 'engage extroverts but drain introverts'. From early childhood, introverts are made to feel out of place – that there's something wrong with them and that their reticence to engage with the world needs to be overcome. Olsen Laney partly blames modern psychology for this, with even Sigmund Freud (an extravert) theorizing that 'psychological fulfilment' is only possible for those engaging with the outside world. Freud saw introversion as unhealthy – even pathological – although he was countered by the more introverted Jung.

Yet we should also suspend our verdict that extraversion is a must for confidence. Olsen Laney is keen to point out that being introverted is not the same as being shy (see Part Four). It's simply a temperament. And a preference for solitude or limited social interaction doesn't make us a 'loner', says Olsen Laney, who considers that self-reflection, an eye for detail and an ability to focus are virtues that should be celebrated. According to Olsen Laney, introverts succeed as often as extraverts, even in areas – such as acting – where extraversion is viewed as vital. She cites Grace Kelly and Clint Eastwood, and even the comedian Steve Martin, as famous introverts, potentially utilizing their introversion to succeed in fields full of extraverts.

Extraverts are adrenaline-driven

Brain chemistry can impact our predisposition on the extravert–introvert scale, says Olsen Laney. Chemicals such as dopamine, adrenaline and acetylcholine regulate blood flows to the brain, with major differences recorded between the chemical balances and resultant blood flows. Introverts are acetylcholine-driven, which increases blood flow to areas of the brain handling internal needs such as memorizing, problem-solving and planning. Extraverts, meanwhile, are dopamine- and adrenaline-driven, which increases blood flow to areas of the brain involving external processing – including sights, sounds, sensations and tastes.

These chemical differences in the brain result in extraverts having what Olsen Laney describes as a 'full-throttle' nervous system, which spends energy liberally, while introverts have a 'throttle-down' nervous system that conserves energy. The full-throttle system leads to more 'fight or flight' responses, she claims: increasing heart rate and blood flow away from the brain, which – in social situations – can land extraverts in trouble, usually witnessed with horror by introverts.

Indeed, introverts can make extraverts uncomfortable, and *vice versa*. The caution and deliberateness of the introvert can make the incautious extraverts feel they are being judged. Meanwhile, the introverts' slower and more thoughtful speech contrast with extraverts, who often 'speak their mind', sometimes thoughtlessly, which can potentially offend introverts. And this can have a major impact on partnerships: an introverted male may feel overpowered by an extravert female, while an introverted female may consider herself ignored by an extravert male. Meanwhile, two extraverts may compete for external attention while two introverts can become insular – drifting away from group activities and even from each other.

A socially-disabling temperament

Yet for all the measured stoicism of the introvert, we're still faced with the fact introversion is a socially-disabling temperament that can detrimentally impact our self-esteem and sap our confidence. According to Olsen Laney, if introverts want to get ahead they must therefore be prepared to get beyond their comfort zone – especially in social situations (including workplace interactions) – while retaining the advantages of the introvert.

Suggestions include the following (with some thoughts of my own):

- *Have quiet confidence.* Be aware that, as an introvert, you're likely to have skills, capabilities and talents well in excess of the noisy extraverts around you. This should offer you quiet confidence (a sense of satisfaction) rather than noisy arrogance or hubris, although – as an introvert – hubris was never a likely outcome.
- *Listen.* Also be aware that your ability to focus on a particular area and to concentrate makes you a strong listener – a vital requirement in any social situation (see Part Four). Extraverts are too busy talking to listen – despite the fact listening is one of the key social needs for advancement according to writers such as Dale Carnegie in *How to Win Friends and Influence People* (1936): advantage introvert.
- *Observe.* Be the one that notices details with people and things – perhaps the efforts of a host or a friend's new haircut. Again, Carnegie would approve. Extraverts tend to race through a social occasion, noticing little but their own input. The introvert, meanwhile, notices more and therefore enjoys more.
- *Be aware.* But also be aware of the extrovert – perhaps spotting the social landmines he or she has missed and may step on, allowing the introvert to deftly navigate the extravert away from disaster. Even if they don't spot it (or accept the danger) – just about everyone else will.
- *Be the original thinker.* Conversation subjects are often dictated by the extravert but they have no monopoly in this respect – and the amusing aside or googly (a cricketing term meaning a spinning ball that's difficult to play) can often be the one that has everyone appreciating your wit or wisdom. That said, sharp put-downs of extraverts often backfire (undermining your confidence), so are worth avoiding.

Social setting significant for confidence

Yet confidence also comes from being on the right side of the social equation with respect to expectations of extraversion (or otherwise). If the prevailing culture celebrates extraversion, then introverts are likely to add being stigmatized to their already acute feelings of awkwardness, although this can also have an impact the other way around. Indeed, I have sometimes considered myself a natural extravert, although one at odds with my social surroundings as a child. Like most English people brought up prior to the 1980s, my upbringing was geared towards the banishment of extraversion, or 'showing off' as it would have been labelled, which – of course – would have added yet another layer of confusion and isolation to an already under-confident outlook.

So there's no right and wrong side of the extravert–introvert axis for those looking to gain confidence. While extraversion may aid courage, introversion supports self-efficacy: both constituent requirements for confidence. The best outcome may therefore be to decide where along the extravert–introvert axis you belong, accept it and focus on the benefits of that position.

What's Stopping You Being More Confident? *Courage is having the ability to act despite fear, which is possible through techniques such as 'desensitization' and through strong motivation. Introverts may feel disabled in the confidence stakes but, in fact, have many advantages.*

8

TRUST AND JUDGEMENT

As any thesaurus will tell you, trust and confidence are inter-changeable words. Yet the trust we're concerned with here deals with our relationships. It means having inner confidence with others. In this respect, trust is a vital building block for confidence – not least because distrust destroys our confidence more effectively than just about any other external consideration.

Trust is certainly a challenging area for me – at first being overly trustworthy (perhaps emotionally over-investing in a particular person) before swinging wildly towards distrust, almost as if their actions confirmed my unconscious conviction that betrayal was inevitable. Such volatility has been a feature of both my work and personal lives, and has destroyed many friendships and partnerships over the years: again, adding to those layers of confusion and isola-tion that constitute the under-confident person's mental make-up.

Nonetheless, I'm right in one respect. Trust is important.

'Trust is the glue of life,' says Stephen Covey in *The 8th Habit* (2004). 'It cannot be faked and [genuine trust] is rarely produced by a dramatic one-time effort.'

Covey talks of relationships as an emotional bank account that has both deposits and withdrawals, and has trust as its currency. If we try and understand someone we're making a deposit, while seeking their understanding is a withdrawal. Apologizing (for any-thing) is a deposit, as is forgiveness. Pride, deceit and holding grudges are all withdrawals.

Make too many withdrawals and we go into overdraft. Keep withdrawing and the account may close, or our creditors may seek redress – perhaps by raiding our other relationship bank accounts (i.e. by undermining our standing within the group). We should therefore seek to remain in credit – adding to each relationship bank account so it flourishes, which will have a beneficial impact on our confidence.

The scales of trust

Covey's analogy is not for everyone, but it makes an important point: trust from others requires that we are – *first* – trustworthy. We must behave in ways that generate trust before we expect others to trust us or be trustworthy themselves.

Potentially, this is a major barrier for the under-confident, not least due to their past, which is likely to be filled with examples of (often self-perceived) betrayed trust. Yet by changing our direction of travel – by offering trust and being trustworthy before asking for trust or expecting trustworthiness – we can start to undermine the contrary evidence caused by our negative experiences.

At least that's Covey's contention, although many under-confident people will remain sceptical – perhaps because the confident people they know are those that rarely deposit and constantly withdraw from their relationship bank accounts. Of course, we may not be witnessing confidence in the other person but a well-disguised under-confidence. And we may also be considering trust as an inelastic concept, and therefore one likely to snap at the first perceived betrayal. Certainly, that's the view of 'change consultants' Dennis S. Reina and Michelle L. Reina. They take a more pragmatic approach in *Trust and Betrayal in the Workplace* (1999) – stating that our capacity to trust falls along four key scales:

1. *Idealistic-pragmatic.* Being idealistic means having blind trust (sometimes called faith), while being pragmatic means having

more calculated trust. Low confidence often means we're idealistic in our trust, which makes it brittle. We trust too much, too blindly, and then lose trust entirely once our unrealistic expectations are disappointed (this is certainly my experience).

2. *Concrete-abstract*. Concrete trust requires solid and tangible evidence prior to trust. It's suspicious of others and needs that suspicion to be dealt with upfront – making others prove they're trustworthy. Abstract trust, meanwhile, accepts ambiguities and uncertainties, and that there are no general rules with respect to trust. With abstract trust, each person is trusted until events *prove* otherwise.

3. *Simple-complex*. Simple trust sees the world in black and white. Complex trust, meanwhile, notices the shades of grey and perceives the many different aspects of one person.

4. *Undifferentiated-differentiated*. Similarly, undifferentiated trust views groups of individuals (perhaps all men or all Christians) as trustworthy or otherwise. It generalizes, often negatively. Differentiated trust, however, looks at individuals and makes finer distinctions within groups.

From the dynamic above it's easy to conclude where the under-confident person goes wrong with respect to trust. All too often we're idealistic (investing too much in faith/trust), we seek concrete proof prior to trust, and we see things in black and white, and in undifferentiated – i.e. generalized – terms. Sustainable (and therefore confidence-building) trust, meanwhile, comes from being pragmatic, from accepting the ambiguities and complexity of trust, and from refusing the notion of generalizations.

Dealing with betrayal

Of course, a major aspect of trust – certainly for me – is in rebuilding trust after a real or perceived betrayal. These are the moments that destroy our capacity for trust – undermining our confidence, not least because it's external: it's our trust in others that's been destroyed, removing our autonomy and attacking our sense of security.

'Betrayal, like a migraine headache, is energy-depleting and can shut down a whole system,' write Reina and Reina.

Yet we're not powerless. According to Reina and Reina there are seven steps to healing (again, with some thoughts of my own):

1. *Recognize what's occurred and acknowledge it.* Any solution is impossible while in denial.
2. *Accept and absorb the pain.* Yes, grieve your loss. What's happened is upsetting, so be upset. But there are limits with respect to both time and depth – and we need to think about the boundaries to prevent our pain disabling our future actions.
3. *Get support.* Talk it through with trusted peers, although beware of your potentially-subconscious aim of building coalitions against the subject of your betrayal.
4. *Reframe the experience.* At the very least it's taught you a lesson, although try and be objective in this respect. For instance, the lesson should not be of undifferentiated distrust. Distrusting all men/women, or all bosses/employees is a ridiculous and self-harming position, even if you've had a 'run of bad luck' with that group.
5. *Take responsibility.* Admit where you contributed to the betrayal – perhaps with over-promising, unrealistic expectations or ambiguous messaging.
6. *Forgive.* Both yourself and your protagonist, as well as anyone tangentially involved. Of course, this may take time, but recognizing now that – at some point – forgiveness is essential, will help accelerate the process. It will also help avoid adopting those 'rules for life' (as discussed in Part One) that harm the under-confident through their intransigence.
7. *Set new rules.* Establish your rules for acting differently in future, although avoid setting standards that force both you and others to the extremes of the trust-scales.

Yes, yes – all very well in theory. The reality may be too painful to contemplate, at least immediately. Yet there's one golden rule we can apply when considering trust: communication. Nearly always, lost trust becomes a monster inside us – feeding us exaggerated information regarding the extent of the loss and the damage done to our well-being. It's these messages that need to be challenged – not by refutation but through communication with the other party. If we shut down the channels, we're confirming our worst fears: perhaps because that's the view we want (making the resulting loss of confidence self-inflicted).

The bias of judgements

Of course, my problems with trust have had an impact on another part of the confidence puzzle: judgement. Lost trust can destroy our judgement, meaning we make potentially harmful but self-fulfilling decisions based on our insecurities and fears.

The concept of self-fulfilling judgements is what's known as 'confirmation bias' – the tendency for people to favour information that confirms their preconceptions while potentially ignoring or discounting information that could challenge these assumptions.

Just about everyone indulges in confirmation bias, which for very confident people often leads to 'wishful thinking' – that they are luckier or more skilled than they are. This is at least a (mostly) beneficial self-deception, although may encourage self-harming behaviour such as an addiction to gambling or taking poorly-judged risks.

The under-confident, however, have the opposite problem – that confirmation bias wrecks our judgement and destroys our ability to act. This confirmation bias is at play in everything we do. Go into a shop with the self-belief we're an unworthy customer, and the instant the assistant fails to show us strong-enough attention (perhaps due to being distracted) we judge them as having confirmed our low status.

Confirmation bias even harms our memories of past events, making us rewrite our own histories to conform to our potentially-negative self-view – even running old encounters through a new prism or bias fed to us by later conditioning.

Perhaps the most damaging use of confirmation bias (at least externally) is racial stereotyping – observing a particular ethnic group and only noticing those elements that confirm our preconceived ideas of that group. Yet such biases can also work within tight-knit groups and even within groups of friends, especially when someone within the group irritates (see Part Five for more on prejudice).

Heuristics in decision-making

Confirmation bias is what's known as a 'heuristic'. Otherwise called 'rules of thumb', these are mental short cuts everyone uses to speed up judgements. Yet they're also where things potentially go wrong for the under-confident. As the confirmation-bias heuristic shows, we may use our negative self-beliefs to make decisions that confirm these poor convictions, although awareness is an important step towards preventing such biases disabling our judgement.

Another heuristic potentially skewering our judgement is the 'representative heuristic', which deals with biases when categorizing (perhaps random events or probabilities). Psychologist Scott Plous explains the 'representative heuristic' in his 1993 book *The Psychology of Judgment and Decision Making* by using the example of Linda, who is 'committed to social justice'. When a research group is asked to decide what's more likely: 'Linda is a bank teller' or 'Linda is a bank teller *and* an active feminist' the majority pick the second option. While there are inevitably more bank tellers than there are feminist bank tellers, respondents have picked up on the words 'social justice' and 'feminist' and made an illogical connection.

A further example of the representative heuristic is a 'gambler's fallacy' that past events change the probability of future results: a classic being the assumption that a run of roulette-wheel reds will continue (or be broken by a black) when the previous results have no influence on the next. Of course, while the confident may assume their luck will continue, the under-confident will use the representative heuristic to support their conviction of poor luck.

The third common heuristic, according to Plous, concerns 'availability' – i.e. the information we use to assess the probability of an eventuality. It's the availability heuristic that keeps people buying lottery tickets because big wins are big news, so they incorrectly assess the likelihood of their own win. And it's the availability heuristic that induces fear of flying, again because crashes are big news and therefore seem more frequent.

Developing critical thinking

Looking beyond heuristics is therefore an important part of developing strong judgement. Yet the world's ever-growing complexity makes this increasingly difficult – leaving us more and more hostage to the knee-jerk (and usually negative) assessments that have been the under-confident person's burden since early childhood. One way round this – at least according to educational psychologists Richard W. Paul and Linda Elder – is to develop the tools for 'critical thinking'.

In *Critical Thinking*, their landmark 2002 book, Paul and Elder describe critical thinkers (i.e. those with strong judgement) as having 'intellectual virtues' that reinforce good decisions. These include humility, courage, empathy, integrity, perseverance, ability to reason, autonomy (i.e. being capable of independent thought) and fair-mindedness. And while this sounds like a tall order for the under-confident person – blighted as they are by a lifetime of poor self-reinforcing judgements – in reality it's little more than the application of Dweck's growth mindset. It's the journey towards good judgement that matters. And this can be rationalized by exploding judgement into its components.

According to Paul and Elder these are:

- *Purpose*. What are you seeking to achieve from a judgement?
- *Point of view*. From what perspective are you currently thinking?
- *Assumptions*. What assumptions are within your current thinking, and should these be examined?
- *Implications*. What are the likely consequences of any judgement?
- *Information*. What information is required and is it at hand?
- *Inferences*. What can be deduced from the information you already have?
- *Concepts*. What 'principles' or 'theories' (or even heuristics) are at play here, and are they worth questioning?
- *Questions*. Indeed, what should you be asking yourself throughout the entire assessment process, and where will questions have to remain unanswered?

This looks like a lot to ask from anyone trying to improve their judgement. Yet critical thinking is in fact a natural process that, according to Paul and Elder, we develop from experience. By adopting the above rationalization we're simply making ourselves aware of the process.

'Critical thinking when applied to decision-making,' say Paul and Elder, 'enhances the rationality of decisions made by raising the pattern of decision-making to the level of conscious and deliberate choices.'

And if this sounds like a treatise for protracted decision-making, perhaps it should. Good decisions are made slowly – not least because rapid decisions are often fearful and reactive.

Judgement's key ingredient: experience

One last thing on judgement, and a saving grace for those feeling they lack it – it gets better with age. In her hit book *The Secret Life of the Grown-up Brain* (2010), science writer Barbara Strauch cites judgement and wisdom as one of the key neurological gifts of aging.

For instance, in one passage she focuses on the work of Thomas Hess, a psychologist at North Carolina State University, who has undertaken dozens of studies into 'social expertise' and concludes that it peaks in midlife (45–60) when we're 'far better than those younger and older at judging the true character of others'.

According to Strauch, this is not just a function of experience, although that helps. It's a function of the longevity of brain cells devoted to navigating the 'human landscape', as Strauch puts it. 'Scanning studies show that parts of the frontal cortex that deal more with emotional regulation atrophy less quickly than other brain sections as we age,' she writes.

This is reinforced by another midlife 'sweet spot' according to Strauch: wisdom. Yes, a cliché, but also a true one – and one vital for the judgement required to improve our confidence. Wisdom is that 'special mix of heart and mind' that – although viewed with suspicion by some neuroscientists – is nonetheless deeply rooted in most cultures. Through learning and experience, most seem to agree (even if anecdotally), our evaluations improve to an almost mystical level.

Strauch cites William James' famous quote that wisdom is 'the art of knowing what to overlook', which I think has a direct link to confidence. By middle age we've learnt the negative consequences of using *all* the information we receive to try and gain an advantage – even if just through passing on negative gossip in order to under-mine a colleague or friend. Yet *not* using such information is what psychologists such as Laura Carstensen and Mara Mather call 'emotional regulation', which – to me – sounds like a strong alter-native description of both wisdom and good judgement; not least because gossiping and bitching are common traits for the under-confident.

What's Stopping You Being More Confident? *Trust is important for confidence but requires pragmatism and the ability to think abstractly, while accepting complexity and differentiation. Judgement requires an awareness of 'rules of thumb' that may corrupt clear decision-making, as well as a growth mindset. It also improves with experience.*

PART THREE

Achievement

9

IDENTITY

The Social Network – the 2010 film about the creation of Face-book – includes a scene in which Napster founder Sean Parker addresses Mark Zuckerberg in a nightclub. Good-looking, well-dressed, drinking expensive cocktails, the über-confident Parker tells the under-confident, geeky, socially-inept Zuckerberg the way the land lies ahead of him. Despite his confidence, however, there's a twinge of regret in Parker's tone when recalling Napster's spectacular rise and fall.

'Napster wasn't a failure,' says Parker. 'It changed music for better and for always.'

Yet he admits it 'p*ssed a lot of people off', which wasn't good business. Nonetheless, it was one hell of a thing – a big, big, achievement.

'The VCs [venture capitalists] wanted to say, "good idea, kid, but the grown-ups will take it from here",' says Parker ruefully.

'But not this time,' he exclaims, leaning towards Zuckerberg. 'This is *our* time. This time you are going to hand them a business card that says "I'm the CEO, *bitch*".'

The scene fascinates me because of what Parker has and what he's trying to give Zuckerberg: confidence. Despite Napster's collapse, it's real confidence – with depth and meaning. It's the confidence that comes *only* from achievement. It's what makes Parker cool, eloquent and heard through the loud music and dim light. It's even what makes him good-looking (although being played by Justin Timberlake helps). He's done it. In that nightclub it's the key difference between them – with Parker saying to Zuckerberg: 'look at me – I'm the future you.'

'This is what achievement looks and feels like,' he's saying. 'Ain't it great?'

Of course, Hollywood doesn't deal in nuances. It paints in primary colours and draws sharp contrasts. But as a shortcut to our core message, it couldn't be clearer: if you want confidence, *get out there and do something*. Achieve. Because nothing can replace the confidence of achievement.

When it comes to confidence, achievement is gold, silver and bronze all rolled into one.

Where the work begins

So is this a depressing statement for the under-confident – who perhaps feel strong achievement is beyond them? It shouldn't be. But they're right to realize that this is where the work begins. Here's where we move from theory to practice: metaphorically swapping our pen and paper for boots and a hardhat.

As stated, no one is going to give you confidence. And it certainly isn't coming out of a book. Sure, there are things you need to know. But there's also a lot you've got to do. And that's the key message from here on: having dealt with our disabling thoughts – or at least understood them – and having established the positive traits of the confident, we must now take action. Because only once you take action and succeed will you gain true, sustainable, confidence. Only then can you – like Sean Parker – know what confidence actually feels like.

Here you are – in Part Three of a five-part book – primed for achievement. Yet you're still standing at the foot of the highest mountain you'll ever climb: wondering whether you'll ever get to the top, especially if – like me – you have a history of low confidence and poor attainment. With determination, endeavour and planning, however, anything's possible. The only way to the top is one step at a time and the only way to make progress is to get going, using what you've got to get there.

The cycle of excellence

'Smart is overrated,' writes psychiatrist Edward M. Hallowell in *Shine*, his 2011 book on achievement. 'Breeding, Ivy League education, sophistication, wit, eloquence, and good looks – they matter, but they're all overrated. What really matters is what you do with what you've got.'

Hallowell is interested in what makes people prosper in the workplace. He's excited by recent discoveries in neuroscience that point to the plasticity of the adult brain, meaning it has a remarkable ability to change – allowing even the most troubled individuals to 'shine'.

Taking a methodical approach, Hallowell outlines five steps in the 'cycle of excellence' that can be applied to those wanting to gain confidence through achievement:

1. *'Select: Put the person in the right job.'* This is a key theme – that no one can achieve their best when doing the wrong thing in the wrong place. Put a champion jockey in a Formula 1 car and they'll crash. And we're no different – making the calculation of where we belong and what we should be doing vital. As we shall see, this partly depends on our identity, as well as our beliefs and values, which we may still be calculating.

2. *'Connect: The most powerful step.'* As stated, the under-confident can find themselves withdrawing from others – operating in ever-decreasing circles that further undermine their confidence. Strong and growing confidence, meanwhile, will only come from expanding our networks (see Part Four). There's no getting away from it – connections matter: even

geeks such as Zuckerberg and Parker needed them in order to succeed.

3. *'Play unearths talent and ideas.'* Hallowell's plea here is for creativity. Achievement comes from thinking differently. This doesn't mean being a rebel. But it does mean being a free thinker, able to unearth strong and original ideas.

4. *'Grapple and grow: making work pay off.'* This simply means learning to cope with the stresses that inevitably follow growth. If you're determined to make progress, you will. But it will throw up new problems that you'll also have to deal with. These include stress (see Part Five).

5. *'Shine: recognition picks up everything.'* Like the philosophical question regarding trees falling over in the forest (if no one's around do they make a sound?) achievement requires recognition from others. Hallowell's plea is for managers (his primary audience) to acknowledge a worker's achievements: publicly, loudly, unmistakably. Yet as individuals this is also true. Achievement has to have some form of external recognition to really count. This isn't to remove our autonomy (which we should assiduously nurture in order to reduce our dependence on others' approval). But it is to accept the human need for a pat on the back from someone other than ourselves – perhaps a mentor or confidante. That said, we remain the key arbiter of our own achievements so benchmarking our own progress is also vital.

Moving towards something positive

But where to begin? Again, we seem to be lost in the theory, although that's because we've yet to calculate our identity, which is preventing us from getting on the right path. As Hallowell states, probably the most common cause of low achievement is being in the wrong place – forced to do the wrong job. And this is a disaster for our confidence because not only are we likely to fail if we're doing something that doesn't suit us, but the low confidence this generates may prevent us ever finding the right path.

In fact, a key danger at this stage is that many of our immediate choices will be focused on escaping our current course, rather than on proactively sourcing the correct road – resulting in a succession of exhausting highs and lows as our elation at tunnelling out of one prison turns to deflation once we realize we've surfaced in another.

This is such a common problem for the under-confident that it must be the most acute focus of our early actions towards confidence. We must find out who we are and where we belong. Only then can we move positively towards something rather than negatively away.

'The importance of analyzing your true identity prior to setting a goal cannot be under-estimated,' writes motivational guru Jim Cairo in his landmark book *Motivation and Goal-Setting* (1998).

In fact, Cairo points to what he calls the 'eight steps to success', which are:

1. Examine your identity
2. Define your values
3. Establish your goals
4. Put together your action plan
5. Examine your motivation
6. Establish discipline
7. Maintain flexibility
8. Reach your outcome.

According to Cairo, such a trajectory cannot be corrupted – hence the need, now, for an acute focus on examining your identity. This isn't something that can be achieved overnight because, frankly, under-confident people are often defined by their lack of identity: or at least their inability to know who they are or what they stand for. Sure, we may have strong opinions, but – as often as not – these are no more than a mask, meaning they collapse once challenged by a more confident person.

How *not* to define yourself

So how do you decide who you are? Cairo's first plea is that we avoid defining ourselves through external objects. Cars, clothes, job titles: all are nice and all can provide a brief frisson of confidence. But spending our life gathering small external confirmations of our status is shallow in the extreme and will generate only a low and brittle form of confidence that will, eventually, reinforce rather than undermine our insecurities.

This is certainly a lesson I've learnt. When starting work at the bank I was astonished by the internal obsession with job titles – not the ones that denoted what we did (such as Head of Logistics) but the ones that denoted our rank (such as Vice President). Soon enough, I fell in with this obsession because it determined how everyone treated me. And while those higher up the rankings had confidence compared to those lower down, in reality they had no more than a fickle prop for disguising their insecurities. For me, true confidence came not from the greasy pole of the corporate hierarchy but from the *achievement* of starting my own business. And each of us must find our equivalent path.

Yet there are far shallower examples than job titles. I can remember an evening drink at a pleasant marina-side hotel-bar in Connecticut – slightly ruined by the bronzed and arrogant yacht owner lording it over others as he admired his sizable cruiser moored just by the outdoor bar. He was clearly confident: he certainly sounded and acted it, as of course he should – just look at the size of his toy in the harbour! But then, to his horror, a yacht glided in so large that it loomed over his pathetic craft like a swan over a moorhen. He quietened down: his smile now fixed, his tan a little faded. And when the owner of the larger boat blanked him, he excused himself and sulked off back to his now diminished craft – presumably to privately curse his poverty.

What's my point? That yachts are nice to own, but using them to define us – as a crutch for our confidence – is a recipe for exacerbating rather than eradicating our insecurities? In fact, like the desire to stop being under-confident, it's little more than a negative goal: a painkiller rather than a platform for growth.

The stereo-trap

Another identity trap, according to Cairo, is hiding behind a defining label or stereotype: that we are a wife, a father, a son, or even a provider or giver. This can extend to any stereotype: that we are black (in a largely white society) or Scottish (while living in England), or working class (though now a professional). Again, this may be initially comforting or beneficial – a shortcut perhaps that allows others to pigeonhole us (a key human need, it seems). But it's potentially limiting, not least because most stereotypes are based on negative generalizations.

Certainly, this is a trap I've fallen into (far more than material definitions). While concerned by the negatives of the 'Essex boy/ man' stereotype, I've hidden behind it often enough for me to find it convenient. And to this day I love being described as 'George's Dad' or 'Eddie's Dad' – with all the positive and warming connotations it conjures. Yet both can act as an alternative to developing the real me, which only comes from a deep and considered examination of who, exactly, I am and what, exactly, I stand for.

This is not an easy task, as you can see from the fact so many people rely on identity shortcuts via material goods or stereotypes. Even Cairo's suggestion – that we write down our answers to the following questions – has its limits (although remains a worthwhile exercise):

- When thinking about myself, what am I proud of?
- How would my best friend describe me?
- What are the three most important areas of my personal life?
- What are the three most important job functions I perform?
- How would I describe my 'ideal' career?
- Does my current job allow me to express my true identity?
- Do my co-workers view me in the same way I view myself?
- How would I restructure my current job?

In my view, the inadequacies of the above questions are all too apparent, which is not a criticism of Cairo – more a recognition of how hard it is to pin down your identity. And this means you shouldn't expect a full-on, worked-through identity to simply jump out at you at this stage (and certainly not from answering a series of limited questions). As stated, this is a journey, not a destination, and such an exercise is here to help set the compass, although one that will need correcting as we make progress.

Define our values

Given this, Cairo's exercise is a useful start, as long as we can move it on to the next stage, which is to define our values. For Cairo this is an 'essential step in creating meaningful goals'. We must calculate our fundamental beliefs in order to construct the foundations and structure for our endeavours. Otherwise, says Cairo, our life will not be 'in sync', meaning we will essentially be living a lie, with a strong likelihood of a confidence-sapping reckoning once it's revealed as such.

Cairo suggests looking at the following list and ranking each item from 1 to 10:

- Security
- Relationship with spouse
- Fame

- Happiness
- Owning your own business
- Respect of peers
- Wealth
- Relationship with children
- Job/career
- Friendship
- Long life
- Spiritual fulfilment
- Good health
- Relationship with family
- Power
- Retirement
- Travel
- Charity.

What five values ranked highest, asks Cairo? It's these that should receive 80 percent of our time and should form the core of our goal-setting (see below), as well as drive our actions towards achievement.

Principles rather than values

Yet there's a danger here – and one Stephen Covey is alive to in *Seven Habits of Highly Effective People* (1989).

'A gang of thieves can share values,' writes Covey, 'but they are a violation of the fundamental principles. . . . Principles are the territory. Values are maps.'

What Covey means by this is that values are invaluable in helping you set goals, but – if they are not founded on strong principles – may set you along the wrong path.

And while Covey can seem preachy – perhaps too moral for someone looking to gain confidence (and may be prepared to compromise their principles to do so) – he's convinced that only principled behaviour can help you develop permanent and enduring confidence, rather than the flaky and fragile confidence of those using material wealth or job titles as their prop.

In fact, Covey sees such principles as self-evident.

'They exist in all human beings,' he claims, 'regardless of social conditioning' although he admits they may have been submerged through poor experiences. He includes principles of fairness, integrity and honesty, as well as human dignity and even excellence.

'One way to quickly grasp the self-evident nature of principles is to simply consider the absurdity of attempting to live an effective life based on their opposites,' says Covey. 'I doubt that anyone would seriously consider unfairness, deceit, baseness, uselessness, mediocrity and degeneration to be a solid foundation for lasting happiness and success [and certainly not confidence].'

As previously seen with the boat owner in the Connecticut harbour, pursuing shallow or unprincipled values may offer a short-term aid to our confidence (although one easily refuted). But so do cocaine and alcohol, and no one's suggesting these are strong aids for sustainable confidence. And this means Covey's advice – though difficult to swallow – remains relevant. We cannot remove ethics from our need for achievement because, even if unethical achievement initially works, it'll do nothing for our long-term confidence. Instead, we'll spend our life hiding from the reality that we're frauds and that our confidence has been acquired through subterfuge.

What about Zuckerberg?

So where does that leave Zuckerberg and Parker, both of whom could be accused of jettisoning principles in order to win achievement? Napster, after all, was a website sometimes described as music piracy, while – as *The Social Network* points out – Zuckerberg was only one protagonist behind the Facebook idea, which, according to the film, was being propagated by several groups and Zuckerberg associates on the Harvard campus around that time.

In fact, the movie provides the answer to both: Parker's venture failed (hence his sense of regret in the scene described earlier), although he was at pains to point out the beneficial impact his invention had on the music industry (which from this distance is undeniable). And Zuckerberg's battles with others who may or may not have also had the idea, or may or may not have helped him, have been the stuff of legend (and is the main focus of the film). Ultimately, both had to face their demons with respect to their principles, and expensively come to terms with them – making principles an inescapable requirement for achievement.

As we pursue our goals for achievement, therefore, we must ensure that our principles remain a primary concern. At this stage, however, we simply need to articulate them – usually by writing them down (perhaps in our diary). For instance, my principles include a belief in self-improvement (Dweck's growth mindset, no less), a concern for fairness – i.e. making gains by honest means – and a desire to make amends when I screw up, which I do frequently.

And I just need to ensure my goal-setting is compatible with these principles. Either that or I accept they're not my principles at all, which means that I either have to rethink my principles or realize that, no matter what my achievements, they will fail to give me confidence.

What's Stopping You Being More Confident? *When it comes to confidence nothing beats achievement, although this is where the hard work starts. You must first decide who you want to be, avoiding identity traps such as material wealth or job titles. For the under-confident to achieve, however, strong principles are crucial.*

10

GOALS

Ask what I do for a living and the official answer is 'run a public relations company'. Ask what that involves and one of its most important aspects is teaching young graduates to write strong copy – a process I enjoy because it gives me a sense of achievement and therefore boosts my confidence.

But my point here is about what I teach them, which centres on the importance of structuring. Such is the power of presenting your case within a logical, dynamic and compelling framework, well-structured articles can even bring mediocre prose alive. And the same is true in our quest for achievement. Structuring is so crucial – especially for the next stage in our journey, which is defining our goals – that it can help overcome other weaknesses in our goal pursuits (such as poor confidence).

As with those articles, our goals need a central objective that runs right through them. This is our key achievement that every element needs to work towards. They also need a compelling narrative in which our actions are arranged in an order that generates a dynamic – almost inevitable – path. And finally there's what's known as the 'inverted pyramid'. In an article this is the upfront signalling of our conclusion: reversing the school essay trajectory of introduction/body/conclusion by stating right at the start how our article concludes before spending the following paragraphs proving our case. Of course, this is the perfect analogy for our goal-setting, which requires us to state the final outcome before plotting the path towards it.

Creating our *blueprint*

In fact, we should combine the two pursuits and write an article about our goals: what we intend to achieve and how we intend to achieve it. This is our *blueprint*, a written document that we *must* produce if we're to win confidence via achievement. Only once we have an accurate and detailed outline of what our achievement looks like can we hope to turn it into reality.

Certainly, achievement is impossible without goals. These must adhere to our principles, support our values and offer us a long-term vision of our future. And then our *blueprint* must fill in the space between now and our perceived destiny: not only outlining what the final achievement looks like but making sure our every action is the obvious next step towards its fruition.

Begin with the end in mind

Despite this somewhat creative analogy, I'm far from alone in propagating the inverted pyramid when goal setting. In *Seven Habits of Highly Effective People*, Stephen Covey's version is to 'begin with the end in mind' (his second habit).

'To begin with the end in mind means to start with a clear understanding of your destination,' he writes. 'It means to know where you're going so that you better understand where you are now and so that the steps you take are always in the right direction.'

Covey adds that 'to begin with the end in mind is based on the principle that all things are created twice. There's a mental or first creation, and a physical or second creation to all things.'

The mental creation is vitally important for the under-confident because many will have responded to the classic question – 'what do you want?' – with the reply: 'confidence'. Yet this is a negative goal, because the real answer is 'to stop feeling under-confident'. And, although sincere, such a wish is ineffective because it moves us no closer to a tangible, confidence-building achievement.

Avoiding empty actions

Covey warns against empty victories – success without any consideration of the destination, which will be quickly discounted as meaningless. Sure, progress may energize us for a time, but it won't sustain us through the inevitable setbacks because, as Covey states, 'we are leaning our ladder against the wrong wall'. This makes every step a step in the wrong direction – something we may only realize years into our journey, which will be a disaster for our long-term confidence.

By beginning with the end in mind, therefore, we're forcing a deep and immediate evaluation on our goal-setting so that we understand what meaningful and sustainable achievement means *for us*. We must ignore achievement for its own sake – power or money or influence perhaps – because those pursuits are unquenchable. Such directionless attainments do not offer us confidence because there are always those with more power, more money and more influence. Like levels in a computer game, success by this measure takes us deeper into the labyrinth of our own insecurities, which will undermine rather than support our confidence.

Instead, we must concentrate – not on the baubles of achievement – but the substance: not on Sean Parker's swagger or model girlfriend but on his industry-changing invention. It's our version of Napster that we need to find: our participation in the world and its successful outcome, not the trinkets offered to anyone with the money to pay for them.

Using NLP for goal-setting

Again, all just theory perhaps. The future is unknowable, so imagine what exactly? Indeed, this book cannot provide the answers, which you have to find for yourself, although it can tell you where to seek help if you're still struggling to fill in the blanks with a coherent plan.

Probably the most famous goal-setting technique available uses neuro-linguistic programming (NLP), which is an approach to personal development invented in the 1970s by Richard Bandler and John Grinder. NLP has since grown to dominate much of the self-help industry (whether the industry admits it or not). However, like Primal Therapy (mentioned in Part One) it's come under attack as a psychotherapy fad, with little clinical evidence regarding its effectiveness in treating the mental disorders (such as phobias and depression) that it claims to alleviate. Certainly, I think any therapy claiming to cure hardwired insecurities is in danger of over-promising, although it's only NLP's approach to goal-setting being considered here.

According to UK-based NLP expert Robbie Steinhouse, writing in *How to Coach with NLP* (2010), goal-setting should include the following (with some thoughts of my own):

1. *Positive goals.* Steinhouse is agreeing with the notion that goals should move us towards a positive rather than away from a negative (hence 'wanting confidence' being a negative goal). But he also states we should go deeper still and take any positive desires to the next level by asking: 'why is that important to you?' Some 'wants' (such as yachts) are merely props to remove our insecurities, making their attainment, again, no more than a negative desire.

2. *Goals that are sensory-specific.* This is NLP at its strongest – asking us what, specifically, we will see, hear and feel (and even smell and taste) when we achieve our goal. This is called the 'as if' frame – the visualization of our achievement that provides our clearest navigational tool. NLP coaches suggest we spend time with our eyes closed and mind entirely focused on visualizing our future, perhaps in 10 years' time. But, again, avoid visualizing only the mere tokens of success. Think about the achievement itself – what our pursuits look like: our office, colleagues, workday environment and daily activities. If you're having trouble avoiding thinking about the trinkets, why not

think about an industry award worth winning – at least it's relevant to your achievement?

3. *Self-maintaining goals.* Achievement is only possible once goals are both self-starting (i.e. there's no insurmountable barrier preventing commencement – we just need to 'act') and self-maintaining – meaning the journey can be broken into a series of practical steps that can be dealt with in sequential order. These steps need to be planned, resourced and then taken (see Chapter 11).

4. *A timescale.* Without a timeframe, goal pursuits will quickly lose momentum, claims Steinhouse. The next chapter will deal with this in more detail (focusing on immediate time-related goals), yet it should be noted here that care is required when it comes to time-based milestones. If we're too strict with the timeframe, we may make major alterations to our plans when they're on the brink of fruition. Timescales are benchmarks, no more. They're not cut-off points forcing change as the guillotine falls. It's the direction of travel that matters, as well as the broad pace of progress. Remember, the *Titanic* struck an iceberg because the captain pushed the ship too hard (despite knowing the risks) – when it was already on course to reach New York in good time.

5. *Context.* Steinhouse uses the example of King Midas and his failure to inject context into his wishes. 'If he'd wished that everything he touched turned to gold between the hours of 6 p.m. and 7 p.m. on Monday, his story would have been very different,' he opines. By this meaning, context can be no more than the addition of specifics to a general desire: the what, when, where and with whom? Yet the desire for a yacht equally lacks context, making it no less problematic despite being specific. Here we need to add the question 'why?' If the answer is that it will 'give me confidence', then we already know the yacht's limitations in this respect.

6. *What do we keep?* Steinhouse raises an interesting point here – the fact that, as we move away from our present situation,

we may lose some of our current advantages. Indeed, such advantages may be enough to make us hesitate or even postpone our goal pursuits. Quitting smoking is a classic example, with many smokers liking the weight-control benefits of tobacco addiction, although more substantial examples can include the camaraderie of a junior role in the workplace or the low stress levels of non-managerial positions. This is sometimes described as fear of success, and it needs to be tackled head on if we're not to spend the journey pining for what we've just lost – potentially sabotaging our progress. Steinhouse suggests we divide these positives into 'must haves' and 'would likes'. We should look to replace the 'must haves' with another positive that supports our progress, while the 'would likes' can be resisted through a focus on the benefits of our new course.

7. *The price.* This comes down to three potentially-disabling questions. First, there will be costs involved (financial and otherwise). Are we prepared to pay them? Second, the goal will take time to achieve (that could be spent on other projects). Are we happy to spend our time this way? Third, in terms of our 'sense of self' (meaning our values and principles), do we think this goal achievable? Honesty may elicit a 'no' from any one of these questions, which means we may have the wrong goals – based on values we do not truly prize or principles we do not, in truth, hold. And while this may mean we need to rethink our goals, at least we discovered this at the start of the process (rather than several years down the line).

8. *Goals that create a new script.* For the under-confident, this is a key requirement. We need to use goals to override the old scripts – those that (from Part One) chained us to the floor of under-confidence. Of course, if we're moving towards something that – after deep and thoughtful evaluation – we calculate will generate the sense of achievement vital for supporting our confidence, then a new script will emerge. We'll have the courage to act, and can make judgements based on our positive pursuits rather than our negative insecurities. In fact, virtually

all the attributes of the confident should come to the fore with the right goals: optimism (because we're travelling a road we believe in and therefore assume possible), talent (because we're prepared to put in the work to develop our skills beyond the level of competence), self-efficacy (because our competence will encourage our self-belief), resilience (because the knowledge we're on the right road can help deal with the barriers), trust (because our openness to others is a by-product of our positivity towards the future) and even extraversion (because – of course – our confidence blossoms as we grow).

Extrapolate your desires

Still having trouble? It's not easy. Realizing that the key need for confidence is achievement – and that this requires a *blueprint* that not only outlines what's possible (given an extended timeframe) but is detailed and even visualized – is a potentially daunting prospect. To help, here are my own thoughts on goal-setting:

1. *Extrapolate your desires.* Of course values are important and you need to write them down and adhere to them (and realize that those you cannot adhere to, you perhaps don't value). But desires are also important. You have to do something that captures your fascination or your motivation will quickly wane. What subjects interested you at school? Or in the news or on TV? Who are your heroes? Are you creative or technical? Mathematical or linguistic? Interested in humans or things (or animals or concepts)? Take note of these interests because achievement requires endeavour, and hard work feels a lot easier when focusing on what interests you and what you enjoy.
2. *Do your research.* If you're good at something you enjoy, your chances of achievement rise exponentially. Yet others may warn you against your desires – saying 'artists are always poor' or something similar. Of course, the stock reply is 'I'm not inter-

ested in money', which is fine for now. This may change, however, so it's worth doing the research and finding out how your desires can provide a sustainable career path. For instance, art is a major industry with a range of opportunities – not just in producing art but in galleries, retail, printing, publishing, licensing, fairs and exhibitions, private or public procurement, storage, restoration, commercial use, journalism, or as an alternative investment (and I'm sure to have missed a few). Indeed, there are satisfying and profitable careers within each area (sport, fashion, music, drama) – so research them thoroughly and develop your *blueprint* accordingly.

3. *Turn it into a business plan.* Why not take this to the next level and turn your *blueprint* into a personal business plan? So you want a career in art and have perhaps alighted upon the potential for selling works from new artists to major corporations as an investment (and to brighten boardrooms and lobbies)? Great! But first understand the industry: the numbers involved, the major buyers, their proclivities and tastes (and budgets), and the incentives and motivations. Also, who's already doing it – not just the leaders, but *all* those in this sector? Soon, the opportunities for long-term achievement will present themselves – all using your desires as a goal but your research as the means for achievement.

4. *Write it down.* This is imperative. You must record your desired achievement, not just imagine it. Of course, your *blueprint* can be in any format you prefer – not just written words but perhaps a sketch or diagram or even a photograph. As a former journalist, I'm obviously going to suggest a well-structured article format. Yet, even here I may be expressing the limits of my creativity (certainly my architect wife would think so). But whatever the format, express it on paper. And I mean on paper – electronic files get lost or forgotten (although print-outs are fine).

5. *Blueprints get amended.* There isn't a successful *blueprint* in history that didn't require amendment prior to execution – as

well as during construction, testing and even after launch. Yet there are plenty of unsuccessful ones that failed because the designers were too rigid in their approach or incapable of adding to their initial vision. Inventor James Dyson produced more than 5000 prototypes of his revolutionary dual-cyclone vacuum cleaner. And you – too – should show such flexibility: remembering that blueprints are no more than working documents. They're not carved in stone. The second you start – and especially after you've started seeking feedback (another vital need) – you'll almost certainly add nuance and refinement, which is a positive. It means you're on your way.

6. *Use your diary.* The back pages of your diary are perfect for writing your *blueprint* – perhaps the 'final' version after the inevitable and extensive editing. One advantage of using a diary this way is that it forces you to edit your *blueprint* – perhaps down to 500 words. Another is that it remains with you always: something you can even read daily to ensure you remain on track, or reread if you stand at the crux of a difficult decision and need guidance. A third is that it has to be renewed annually, giving you a chance to monitor progress and make amendments. Yet the daily diary is also your friend: your record of the journey, your ledger, your log. It's your confidante as you proceed and your primary tool for feedback – congratulating you on the triumphs and extracting the lessons from your defeats (both of which are inevitable).

7. *'Put first things first.'* This is Covey's third habit and is almost self-explanatory. Becoming an art procurement expert for major corporations is a great long-term goal and an achievement that's sure to give you confidence. But you won't get there in one leap. It'll be a series of steps, so you should find out what the steps are and plan them. One advantage of this is that you lose your fear of the final destination, which – once in the *blueprint* – can be ignored in favour of a laser-like focus on the next step. Like climbing a mountain from a sea-level start, there's no point standing in the waves and worrying

about the final ascent to the peak. Having visualized the mountain and sketched the route, scaling the beach cliff is our only pressing concern – the planning of which is the next stage in our journey.

What's Stopping You Being More Confident? *Goals are vital for achievement because they give ambitions meaning and a focus. Yet goals require a blueprint outlining what the end product looks like. This must be a detailed vision that 'begins with the end in mind'.*

11

THE PLAN

Visualizing mountains is all very well, but unless mountaineering is our desired achievement it's no more than a metaphor. We need to keep things real, and that requires a focus on process – especially with respect to our immediate plans. Indeed, endeavour and process are the two key ingredients for achievement, with one entirely dependent on the other. Hard work without a thought-through plan of execution will waste time and destroy resolve. Meanwhile, all plans and no action – well, that's just dreaming.

My own world of PR offers a potentially useful structure when it comes to planning our immediate actions – not least because our PR projects are guided by a *Campaign Plan*, which details action points and milestones for the year ahead. Such a plan gives the client confidence we know what we're about and a benchmark by which they can measure our success. It also generates momentum. We don't need resolve, or perseverance, or passion or even willpower. We just need to execute the *Campaign Plan*.

Requirements for a *Campaign Plan*

Unlike the *blueprint*, which sets out the ultimate vision (as well as sketches a route for achievement), our *Campaign Plan* is an entirely practical document focusing on the next 12 months. And this usually means adopting the following headings:

1. Mission Statement
2. Objectives
3. Timeline
4. Messages
5. Audiences
6. Strategy
7. Tactics/Actions.

While the headings are self-explanatory, some additional depth may be worthwhile in each case.

1. Mission statement

The aim here is to get your *blueprint* (now written in the back of your diary) down to a single sentence that states your core long-term objective. Of course, it must be memorable – allowing it to be recalled, perhaps when in Sullivan's '*clutch*' or when our resolve may be otherwise flagging. If using our art procurement example, maybe our mission is 'creating a company that connects talented artists with pioneering collectors'. Such a statement is both succinct and self-explanatory. It's also flexible and memorable – making it a compelling one-line declaration of intent for the top of our *Campaign Plan*.

In fact, this can be taken a stage further – reducing it to a phrase or tagline providing, not only the headline for our *Campaign Plan*, but a mantra short enough to be etched on our consciousness and focused enough to compel us into action. 'College art for companies' could work for our example, perhaps, or maybe 'investing in tomorrow's artists', which has the added benefit of being a positive message – encompassing our values – for both us and our audiences (see below on messages and audiences).

But your mission statement doesn't have to précis your *blueprint*. Instead, it can capture the essence of *you* – or at least the person you are striving to be. In times past, this may have been the family motto. For instance, my wife's family motto is *Onward*, which I like for its descriptive brevity (getting a mission statement down to one word is certainly impressive), while I've adopted Winston Churchill's mantra of 'KBO' ('keep buggering on') – because I like the dogged endeavour and sense of embattlement it conjures.

Ships' names – such as *Endeavour* or *Endurance* – have often struck me as good examples, and the occasional corporate strapline (such as 'the world's favourite airline') also manages to achieve that mix of who we are and how we measure ourselves (although – as with 'don't be evil' – this can sometimes become a hostage to fortune). Each morning I cycle past a (now converted) Victorian warehouse complex called *Perseverance Works*, which I also like. Indeed – as with KBO – it can be humorous or a play on words, although it must signify something important and relevant: encapsulating our inner being in a way that's memorable and motivational.

2. *Objectives*

Though dealt with in the *blueprint*, the objectives should now be rewritten with a one-year timeframe – giving you the opportunity to practically re-evaluate them. Objectives that are pursued without vigour or enthusiasm – or perhaps undertaken with an inner conviction of eventual defeat – are pointless. Indeed, they may not even be your goals: perhaps given to you by a parent or teacher or from reading a magazine. They must also be achievable – not immediately but eventually, which makes your one-year objectives a strong benchmark as well as your primary focus. What has to be achieved within the next 12 months for you to know that the changes being made are embedded, supportable and, importantly, moving you towards confidence via strong achievement? As with self-efficacy in Part Two, you must set yourself targets that are ambitious but not beyond your capabilities.

In this respect it may be worth working backwards. Looking ahead as our future stretches over the horizon is almost impossible, because even minor changes can take us way off course (as any navigator can tell you). However, if we – mentally – go straight to our perceived destination, and look back to our current spot, it's far easier to develop an accurate path between the two points.

This is no different to Covey's recommendation to start with the end in mind, although – for your *Campaign Plan* – the 'end' should be no further than your one-year horizon, which can be written as a series of bullet points. For instance, our art example could have the following one-year objectives:

- Company called *Tomorrow's Art Ltd* registered and trading
- 10 promising artists signed and supplying art on an exclusive basis
- Entire customer base researched and approached
- First corporate customer won – and project executed
- Company website and brochure produced, showcasing our first completed project.

One more thing on writing objectives: now is the time to change the language – turning off the negative tapes. As you can see from the above, the objectives are no longer 'goals'. They are milestones. They should therefore be written in present tense language – not that they *will* be achieved but that they *are being* achieved. This isn't an excuse to become a fantasist – unachievable goals will, after all, undermine your confidence. It's simply a statement of intent. Sure there may be bends in the road, but they can be dealt with as they come up. Confidence requires us to be bold, and to trust ourselves, which should be expressed through the plans we execute but also the language we adopt.

3. *Timeline*

Most PR firms put this at the end of the *Campaign Plan*, but for personal statements it's worth bringing forward simply because – as we are building confidence – the order of achievement is crucial. Having stated your one-year objectives you are, again, filling in the blanks between your current and future points. This can even be visual – using a clock face with the hours as monthly milestones: hour/month one – set up the company and complete database of potential customers; hour/month two – sign first artist, etc., which also helps to build in quarterly and half-yearly milestones.

All career or personal fulfilment paths can be dissected in this way in order to generate milestones for indicating that, yes, you are travelling the right path, at the right pace, and gaining confidence as you go. Importantly, you can also see what success looks like, giving the journey that all-important sense of achievement without having travelled very far at all.

In fact, such timelines are probably the most effective way of developing Dweck's growth mindset. The momentum you generate from travelling such a path is sensational because, as you reach a particular milestone, you're already focused on the next. This allows you to acknowledge the fact your achievements are building your confidence, while also observing that there's plenty yet to achieve.

And if you slip – taking three months to reach the two-month mark? So what? The timeline is simply a roadmap to the future – whether you're at point X in month Y or month Y+1 is of little consequence (although be careful not to make such slippage a habit).

4. Messages

For a PR firm, messages are an important part of any *Campaign Plan*. In essence, PR tries to instil positive messages in the minds of significant audiences – allowing clients to be perceived as they wish. Many consider this dishonest. And at its worst, it is. But dishonest messaging is usually found out, undermining campaigns or even voiding them. So messages must reflect our true values and principles if they are to be effective.

In fact, they should be no more than the best expression of our true selves. This is what we want others to mentally conjure when our name is raised. Of course, it needs to be credible – boastfulness will simply set us up for a fall. But it also needs to boost our confidence rather than underline our insecurities. Too often the under-confident resort to self-deprecation when talking about themselves (certainly a trait of mine). But this is usually less about modesty and more about presenting our weaknesses as a virtue, perhaps before they are presented back to us as a fault.

Being achievement-focused is a crucial part of strong messaging as it strips away any general considerations about you as a person. Messages are simply about goals, which should make them easier to write (and negates the need for modesty or self-deprecation). Again, with respect to messages, our art example may clarify:

- We find new and exciting artists, and promote them
- We also promote modern art as an alternative investment for corporations
- We offer good value to art investors, while helping give talented artists a strong start
- We make this an exciting process but one we execute with integrity: after all, trust will be important to both our key audiences.

Also, notice what's *not* included as a message:

- I am a confident person
- I am popular
- I am the best
- I will succeed, come hell or high water
- Have you seen how big my yacht is?

As stated, these messages are 100 percent focused on *achievements*. They are statements of fact, and of intent – perhaps aligning your desired achievements with your core values – not with your insecurities (which boastfulness will reveal) or the mere trinkets of success.

Of course, you cannot force people to think about you this way. But you can at least start the process of thinking about *yourself* this way, which should induce a change in your behaviour. This is important because we're constantly giving ourselves and others messages: in the way we dress, speak, act, interact and respond to others. Our pattern of speech, facial expressions, manners, posture, gait – and just about everything else – are all vital messages regarding who we are and how we expect to be judged (see Part Four). We need to be acutely aware of this – making the writing of messages that are immediately undermined by our behaviour pointless and even damaging. For instance, if we cite integrity as an important message, we have to behave *and think* with integrity. This is a deliberate act, which we've acknowledged by writing it down as a key message.

5. Audiences

Achievement involves other people. It's impossible without them, although dealing with others can be a major failing of the under-confident (see Part Four). All we're doing here, however, is noting the significant others for our achievements. That said, you should aim to look beyond the obvious – clients, customers, bosses, etc. – adding *all* the key audiences involved in any achievement, including those that may be perceived as a barrier to your progress.

Continuing with our art investment venture, audiences will include.

- *The artists.* These are our core suppliers, so there's no achievement without them. We'll need to convince them we are sympathetic to their creativity and can help introduce them to the right buyers' market *for them.* Clumsiness here could be costly.
- *The investors.* But clumsiness here could be equally disastrous. Investors will see the world very differently from artists. Are we able to offer the right messages to both audiences without alienating either party? A key skill for anyone seeking achievement will be navigating these potentially contradictory messages for different audiences.

- *Intermediaries.* But there may be others we need to influence – using specific messages that, nonetheless, need to offer a consistent value-based proposition. For instance, journalists will want to know we have our finger on the pulse, college lecturers that we are acting in their students' interests, suppliers that we can pay the bills etc.
- *Rivals.* An important audience that we cannot ignore, as much as we'd like to. What's our point of differentiation? Our advantage over them? How can we sustain our advantages or mimic theirs? And is there room for partnering?
- *Associates.* People that know us will likely be our greatest allies in the early days when we're trying to bash down doors. However, they may also (secretly) be our deepest critics: potentially sabotaging our progress with unkind words or even just knowing looks and raised eyebrows. Our messaging needs to get as many people onside as possible – not least because achievement is nearly always about making friends, not losing them. This is a key lesson the over-ambitious – including myself at times – need to learn (just ask Sean Parker). As I say to colleagues who are sometimes too feisty in meetings (echoing my earlier behaviour): it isn't about winning but about winning people over.
- *Family.* You cannot run away from your family. Well, you can – but you'll be far more effective if you carry them with you. Some of your messaging, therefore, has to be geared towards your nearest and dearest. Get your family genuinely onside, and you may have won over possibly the hardest audience you'll ever need to persuade. Fail to do so, and your family can quickly become your greatest barrier.

Whether a company or an individual, audiences are therefore important across the spectrum of our desired achievement. Indeed, another Stephen Covey habit is to 'synergize', which means to try and effectively cooperate with as many people as possible – seeking genuine partnerships at all levels. As Sean Parker found out, 'p*ssing people off' is an ineffective way of pursuing any achievement.

6. *Strategy*

I used to struggle with the concept of a strategy, but I now realize it's the pivot – turning plans into effective actions. It's also the element of our *Campaign Plan* that ensures all our actions are the right ones for meeting our objectives.

Given this, strategies are important. But they can be the elements of a *Campaign Plan* that people find hardest to conceive, and certainly struggle to implement. Indeed, many people execute action points or tactics that are not strategic (see busyness below) – meaning there's no certainty such actions are focused on their preferred outcome or geared towards their achievements.

A war analogy offers the simplest example – comparing two twentieth century wars: World War Two and the Cold War. Both had the objective of victory and – for the allies – both involved a totalitarian adversary that they felt posed an existential threat. Yet while WWII involved a strategy of 'total war' (with tactics focused on land, sea and air attacks), the Cold War was a wait-and-see stand-off (involving tactics such as propaganda, an arms race, and pursuing small proxy wars in various post-colonial theatres of combat).

While nervous of over-simplifying history, these opposing strategies were pursued – broadly – because of the strengths and behaviour of the allies' opponents. Nazi Germany was an over-stretched occupying power (as was Imperial Japan) making it vulnerable – especially when considering the productive capacity of the United States. In the Cold War, meanwhile, the Soviet Union possessed nuclear weapons, making a full-on assault potentially suicidal. Yet it was also economically vulnerable, which meant a contain-but-wait strategy may bear fruit over the long term. These different assessments led to very different strategies pursued via different tactics, despite both wars having the same objective: victory.

So we must do the same in order to discover our most effective strategy. What are our strengths and where are our weaknesses? What's an immediate *must do* (not just a *can do*), and what requires some further thought and perhaps some skill-acquisition?

While our art company is, therefore, progressing well – with lots of endeavour – does it have the right strategy: especially in a world where reputation is everything? If we look again at the objectives, our *Campaign Plan* involves a strong year-one attack on the entire art-buying corporate universe – ensuring that all our potential investors know who we are. Yet 'getting known' is just one strategy, and maybe not the right one. Art snobs abound, and art-buying is a village, so any major mistakes while pursing such an extensive strategy may damage us.

Perhaps a better strategy is to find *the* artist – after an intensive search – and discreetly source *one* buyer that totally suits that artist's needs: importantly ignoring any other form of marketing. Word can then 'get round' regarding our 'discovery', making us *the* dealer the key people want to deal with, rather than the one everyone knows yet wonders about.

7. Tactics/Actions

At some point the talking and planning has to stop and we have to act. Well, that point has arrived, although not before we've written another list – this time the 'to do' list of immediate actions in order to meet the one- to two-month milestones. Yet, by now, our needs should be straightforward:

- Make sure we have the equipment we need to meet our immediate requirements
- Ensure our workspace is adequate and primed for action
- Create a database template with the right headings
- Start compiling a 'big list' of potential customers and suppliers
- Go to the Companies House website and fill in the registration form
- Get some stationery printed – including business cards.

And the fact the above list seems so mundane, so matter-of-fact, so – well – obvious, is good news. After all this planning we've broken down our actions into the practical and doable activities that form the DNA of strong achievement. We have reduced a potentially daunting leap into tiny, almost-innocuous, steps.

Avoiding the traps of execution

Yet the day-to-day execution of our plans has pitfalls for the under-confident – hence the need to use our *Campaign Plan* to ensure we stay on track. Traps to avoid include the following:

- *Busyness.* Stephen Covey calls this the 'activity trap': working furiously away on something – anything – and getting a buzz from the energy being generated, while paying little attention to its strategic value. In moderation this is fine – good, even. But straying too far off-plan could simply be a disguised form of procrastination (see Part Five) in which we obsess on the minutia of a particular tactic in order to delay meaningful action (that may, for instance, trigger our insecurities). Our diary should help – using it to record our daily progress and preventing us loitering too long on a particular (perhaps tangential) action.
- *Interruptions.* Dealing with interruptions is one of the most painful aspects of any execution. As Part Four will state, we need to keep other people onside in our endeavours and that means finding the time and energy to deal with their needs as well as our own. Strong timetabling is the only way to accommodate both. Interruptions will usually come from the same people, at the same moments in the week so – through timetabling – we can become proactive and schedule the time: asking them what they need, and when, before they disturb us with their seemingly urgent enquiry. You can then ask for the favour to be returned, with them respecting your need to 'press on'.

Indeed, creating a weekly timetable with hourly slots between 7 a.m. and 7 p.m., seven days a week, is a strong way of regaining control of your time. After all, that's 84 hours a week in which to find time for pursuing the most important project in your life.

- *Derailments.* A key moment in the execution of any plan will be the first setback. If we make a call and get a 'no'; or if we present our idea and win only contempt – what then? Thorough, realistic and well-structured plans can be derailed in this way, or even abandoned. Yet it's no more than one (temporarily) failed action point. Again, use your diary to record any setbacks – focusing on the lesson. Indeed, the next action point can be applying the lesson from the previous failure (although beware of turning your project into a quest for a 'yes' – any 'yes').

- *Cost.* Baulking at the cost is perhaps the quickest, and certainly one of the most common, ways of rendering entire campaigns void. So cost your plans as far forward as you can. Then add 20 per cent as a potential overspend, and – most importantly – be prepared to pay it. And not just money. Time, effort, emotion, tears, humiliation: we need to be prepared to pay the price for our achievements – they do not come cheap in any of these respects. That said, hesitation at this point (when the costs have to be met) may reveal your true motivations (or lack of them).

Yet the most important point of all is that you get going – constantly referring back to the *Campaign Plan* to ensure you're on the right path, as well as making tiny adjustments to various messages or tactics or required resources as you go. Unlike your *blueprint*, this is a working document, something that requires detail and evaluation at every new horizon. At Moorgate (my PR company), we assume such plans allow six months of pro-activity, although we check our progress with the client monthly. At the beginning of month six we re-evaluate the entire campaign – altering our tactics (and perhaps even our strategy) if required. And by the end of month nine, we're with the client planning the objectives, messages, strategies and tactics for year two.

> **What's Stopping You Being More Confident?** *Your blueprint requires a Campaign Plan for at least the next 12 months. This must include your immediate objectives, your key messages, your audiences, a strategy and some tactics for execution. You must then act – avoiding traps such as 'busyness' or being side-tracked by interruptions.*

PART FOUR
Situations

12

SHYNESS

Executing our plans means developing confidence: not in private or on paper, but with real people in real situations. Yet this can trigger shyness for the under-confident – a beguiling trait in children but a disabling one for adults. At the very moments we need to speak, our shyness renders us speechless. Just as we need to move, our shyness roots us to the spot. And when the requirement is for us to act, our shyness tells us to hesitate.

Again, controversy rages regarding the roots of shyness - whether it's innate or something we develop, perhaps via negative early experiences. That said, it could equally be a mixture of the two – maybe with one reinforcing the other.

Certainly, I've always seen my own shyness as incident-related. For instance, I can remember being attacked by a boy called Gary on my first day at Writtle Infants School (making me five) – an event that left me under-confident when dealing with my peers in the playground. While by no means a bold child, I'd started to develop strong friendships – sometimes with older boys – from spending two terms at a much smaller school in Chelmsford. Yet the older boys could play rough, so – at first – I assumed Gary's approach was equally benign. I smiled and laughed as he pushed me against a low wall – comprehending his aggressive intent only after looking up and seeing his contorted face. And, as the blows started raining down on my tiny frame, my confused openness turned to abject terror.

Thanks to Gary, the optimism with which I greeted my new environment disappeared – to be replaced by an outlook more guarded and distrustful. Uncertain how to respond, I became discomforted by any approach and watchful for fear of further attack. And while outwardly this looked like shyness, inwardly it was something far less endearing: fear.

The role of the amygdala

Of course, Gary's attack is unlikely to be the whole story when it comes to my shyness. Yet such incidents are important as they are the formative events for our evaluations of others – the episodes that turn our perhaps open regard for those we encounter into fearful responses triggered by (potentially unconscious) negative memories. As Daniel Goleman writes in *Emotional Intelligence* (1996, citing experts such as Dennis Charney of Yale University), this is no less than a mild form of post-traumatic stress disorder (PTSD): the impact of shocking events leading to anxieties and phobias with respect to social interaction.

Gary's attack is certainly burnt into my memory, as such events will be for us all thanks to the interaction of two key elements of the brain's limbic system. First, the amygdala is triggered. This is the part of the brain dealing with emotions and distress. It signals an emergency to the entire nervous system – flooding the brain with hormones and putting the body on general alert (inducing classic 'fight or flight' responses such as an adrenaline rush, the sweats and shaking). And this makes a deeper impression on the hippocampus, the part of the limbic system – generating long-term memories.

It's the interaction between the amygdala and the hippocampus that triggers our automatic – and fearful – response whenever tangentially reminded of the event. Indeed, many PTSD sufferers develop a condition psychologists call Social Anxiety Disorder (SAD), which – according to the *Diagnostic and Statistical Manual of Mental Disorders* (2000) – has symptoms that include:

- A frequent and unending fear of social situations, especially when coming into contact with unfamiliar people
- Panic attacks at the prospect of encountering such a situation – perhaps looking immediately for an excuse to avoid
- Fear of even appearing anxious or acting in a way that will bring about embarrassment or humiliation.

The bold-timid dimension

For sure, SAD resonates with my own social phobia. Yet others may view their shyness as simply introversion, which – as we have seen – is an innate Jungian personality type, perhaps differentiated from the extravert by nothing more than brain chemical balances altering our emotional circuitry.

At least, that's the finding of psychologists at the Laboratory for Child Development at Harvard University. Led by Jerome Kagan (and described by Goleman), the psychologists studied infant brain patterns in order to plot children along a dimension ranging from boldness to timidity.

'In free play with other toddlers, some were bubbly and spontaneous, playing with other babies without the least hesitation,' writes Goleman. 'Others, though, were uncertain and hesitant, hanging back, clinging to their mothers, quietly watching the others at play.'

Four years later, Kagan's team observed the children again. Now in kindergarten (the start of formal education), the psychologists noted that all the outgoing kids were still confident. Meanwhile, around two-thirds of those viewed as timid remained 'behaviourally inhibited'. According to Kagan, the timidity stretched to anything that wasn't familiar, making them reluctant to eat new foods or to visit new places, although it was most acute around strangers.

'The timid children seem to come into life with a neural chemistry that makes them more reactive to even mild stress,' says Goleman. 'From birth, their hearts beat faster than other infants in response to strange or novel situations. At 21 months, when the reticent toddlers were holding back from playing, heart rate monitors showed that their hearts were racing with anxiety . . . They treat any new person or situation as though it were a potential threat.'

A lower threshold of excitability

Around a fifth of infants fall into the timid category, says Goleman, with an early clue being how distressed babies become when confronted with something unfamiliar. 'Stranger fear' is particularly acute, notes Kagan, with timid children showing high levels of stress if the baby's mother leaves the room while a stranger remains present. One potential reason – says Kagan – is that the baby has inherited high levels of norepinephrine (known as noradrenaline outside the US), one of several neuro-transmitting chemicals that activate the amygdala and lead to a lowering of that child's threshold of excitability. Certainly, higher levels of norepinephrine/noradrenaline were measured in the urine of the timid children within Kagan's study group.

Yet Kagan's timid children revealed other symptoms, including higher resting blood pressure, greater dilation of the pupils and much lower speech levels compared to the bolder children. Indeed, when directly addressed, the usual response of the timid child is to clam up, which – according to Kagan – may be a sign of intense neural activity overriding the brain's ability to vocalize. Raise the temperature of the encounter a notch, and the same circuits cause the child to cry.

And as they grow, sensitive children are at high risk of developing anxiety disorders or panic attacks. External triggers such as intense social situations can generate heart palpitations, shortness of breath or a choking feeling, as well as an impending feeling of disaster. Even as adults, those that were timid children are prone to becoming the wallflowers: disliking parties or becoming terrified when asked to perform publicly or give presentations – even succumbing to guilt and self-reproach due to their self-perceived social failings.

Emotional responses

Goleman's *Emotional Intelligence* is, indeed, a revelatory read for the under-confident. As I turned the pages I began to question my assumptions regarding particular incidents and their impact. Perhaps my earlier analysis was wrong and I'd falsely accused Gary of generating my SAD-style fears. Was I simply filling in the blanks – assuming my social timidity was incident-generated and therefore seeking, and of course finding, the event that best suited that notion?

Maybe I was born this way. I'm told I was a cry-baby – emotionally needier than my sister and certainly more clingy. And right through childhood even mildly-stressful incidents triggered emotional responses in me far more readily than my peers.

To this day, difficult situations trigger a greater emotional response from me than those around me – especially when a situation becomes focused on *me* and particularly when dealing with seemingly-rational or confident people. When accused of something or mildly rebuked, or even just put on the spot, I can become so emotionally triggered that I'm incapable of rational thought. This usually results in silence, which others can mistake as sulking, although is actually a raging inner battle to try and regain control over my emotions. Adrenaline flows, my heart races and any rational thoughts are over-ridden by feelings of bewilderment, anger, anxiety and injustice – making silence a far better option than the only available alternatives: anger or tears.

But social situations are no better. Perfectly happy scenes that I'm expected to enjoy can equally trigger a negative inner response. I can feel panicked – perhaps fantasizing about perceived hostility towards me or assuming I'm not welcome or that I'm disliked or not worthy of the company. I become convinced I've nothing to say or that my views are of no consequence, or simply wrong. Again, rational thought seems beyond me – rendering my utterances, indeed, unworthy when only moments earlier I'd been articulate and capable of intelligent conversation.

Social situations trigger shyness

Far from a beguiling trait, shyness can therefore hide an inner turmoil that produces highly-disabling external responses. Indeed, humans are social animals and the core of our confidence is our ability to interact successfully. Lose here, and just about every door to achievement stays shut. So we have no choice but to improve our social skills, which means we *must* fight our timidity – not least because it's eroding both our well-being and our potential for achievement.

But we need an analytical approach rather than a full-on frontal attack (which may backfire – further undermining our confidence). For instance, we should realize that timidity is usually situational: i.e. triggered at particular points. Few people are shy always and everywhere. So we simply need to expand our universe of comfort to encompass the moments we fear.

For most shy people the most terrifying situation is meeting and mingling with strangers, perhaps at a party or event or a new place of employment. Of course, meeting new people is important – after all, we cannot make progress locked in a closet. Yet these are the moments that make us want to flee, or – at best – cling to the one person we know without once daring to step beyond our comfort zone. And while we can tell ourselves this is an irrational response based on childhood insecurities, it's no less real for that, which means we have no choice but to develop a strategy for overcoming our fears when meeting strangers.

But first let's go easy on ourselves, not least because our shyness is hardly uncommon. According to self-promotion guru Ilise Benun in *Stop Pushing Me Around!* – her 2006 book on workplace shyness – around 40 percent of Americans consider themselves shy, a figure probably exceeded in the UK thanks to our cultural encouragement of introversion.

Such statistics may surprise the shy – especially when surveying social situations in which everyone else seems to be interacting confidently. Yet that doesn't mean the 40 percent have avoided the event. It means that others have managed to get beyond their fears, perhaps by disguising them. As Susan Jeffers would say, they are feeling the fear and interacting anyway – partly because they've adopted a key strategy for success in social situations: they're *not* being themselves.

Don't be yourself

Of course, this runs up against conventional wisdom, which advises the shy to 'just be themselves' when meeting new people. However, social situations are probably the most acute trigger for timidity imaginable, which means 'being yourself' can involve our fears being activated to the point where we think avoidance the only logical response.

At social events, we have to join a room full of hostile-looking strangers and act as if we're enjoying being there – and that means faking confidence. That said, we should avoid adopting a fixed grin and a headlong charge into the crowd (a tactic likely to confirm our convictions of hostility). Instead, we should challenge our assumptions and adopt a strategy for winning people over.

For the timid, Ilise Benun offers the following advice when meeting new people (mixed in with some thoughts of my own).

Don't assume hostility
OK, this is easier said than done. Groups of people engaged in conversation have a habit of signalling their lack of need for your inclusion, making interruptions forced and potentially embarrassing.

But groups look hostile because that's how your brain interprets the situation. A good number will be in Benun's 40 percent and will be feeling as awkward as you. So why not look for them? This means the room could be 90 percent hostile but of no consequence because you're simply seeking the 10 percent that aren't. Surely, even our most fearful interpretation of the situation can accept that not *everyone* in the room is hostile. So find your soulmate – even if it takes you several goes.

Of course, there will always be those that are hostile, or at least see themselves as too important to talk to the likes of you. Fine, although this usually says more about them than you. For instance, whenever I've met truly important people they project an air of sincerity that – of course – may be affected but is nonetheless attentive and welcoming. They listen and give a good impression of being interested – not least because most successful people have a growth mindset. Anyone openly showing disinterest, therefore, is clearly unimportant. Probably insecure, they're scouring the room looking for important people to impress – not noticing the poor impression they're making as they do so.

State the obvious
One introductory gambit that can work is honesty. If you're trying to find a friendly face in a crowd of hostile-looking people, why not say so – not least because the recipient will feel complimented that you've spied them as the friendly face?

In fact, why not start with a compliment or positive remark? This could be to the person you target . . .

'You look like someone worth talking to.'

. . . or about the venue . . .

'What a fascinating room/building/garden.'

. . . the event . . .

'What a fantastic gathering, so well organized.'

. . . or even the drinks . . .

'Great cocktails.'

Anything, in fact, that can project positivity and open a conversation, as well as avoid the 'Hi, I'm John – who are you?' introduction. That said, there's nothing wrong with boldness, though the shy may find such a frontal attack difficult. The line 'can I join your conversation?' is, however, a strong gambit that can have those within scrambling to make you welcome. Yet you need to pick your conversation. If the CEO, CFO and Chairman are intensely engaged, it may be worth finding a less intimidating huddle to interrupt if you're not to immediately trigger your insecurities.

Be curious
You should take your cue from the truly important and develop your listening skills. Indeed, timidity can revolve around the notion that nobody will be interested in *you*. Fine: let's assume you're right and make it about *them* instead. Become curious. Ask lots of questions, and listen to the reply. One trick (adopted by the socially adept) is to develop what's known as 'empathetic listening'. Sometimes called active listening, you're simply using what you're told to deepen the level of conversation. This way, you can even engage potentially hostile or disinterested people.

'Hi, I'm David – Ford Motors,' we say – offering that extra snippet of information in order to illicit the same from them.

'John – Volvo,' could be the curt response.

'What's new at Volvo?' we ask, using an open question (to illicit more than a yes/no reply).

'Plenty,' says John, remaining curt.

'Plenty good or plenty bad?' we ask. 'Certainly Ford has a mixture of the two.'

The add-on here is simply to prevent them feeling grilled. It shows you are happy to offer information as well, which should loosen them up a little – although the conversation is still about *them*.

'Mostly good,' says John. 'Sales of the new model are strong . . . '

. . . and we're off. John's now mentioned sales and the new model – two routes for the empathetic listener to follow (perhaps calculating which is John's primary interest).

Yet there's no need to push it here. If John remains disinterested – well, you've now established the fact he's revealing his lack of importance, so best move on to someone worthy of your attention.

Give good small talk

This is certainly a problem for me. Being a pseudo-intellectual I feel most comfortable indulging myself in some meaningful diatribe about an in-depth subject. Yet not only is this off-putting to those there to meet new people rather than solve global issues, it's also potentially alienating. Meaningful conversations usually involve controversial opinions. And that's a disaster when trying to overcome our timidity by winning people over.

In fact, many overly-serious people are doing no more than masking their insecurities by focusing on depth rather than range when conversing – perhaps trying to steer a conversation towards their specialist area. It's making small talk that takes skill: keeping it light and engaging. Again, compliments help, as does empathetic listening.

Arrive early

Oddly, the timid often delay their arrival at an event – not wanting to be 'the first to arrive'. Yet arriving late will more likely trigger your insecurities. Most conversations will be underway and the pattern of the evening well-established without you. So why not arrive early? This is especially the case if you're keen to meet the host, who'll obviously be less pressured early on (and keener to get the gig swinging).

Certainly, this is now my ruse – not least because, once I've met the host, I'm normally bristling with information, which increases my confidence. I feel like an insider, able to impart knowledge to the late arrivals.

Do your research

Going through an invite list line-by-line can seem a bit intense. But a glance for clues regarding the type of people likely to be at an event – and exploring Google for a few titbits that can be thrown into conversations – can be highly effective. The more you know about the host, and the event, the less you'll feel like you're walking into a jungle full of savage animals. Even if you don't use the information, your confidence will be higher when entering the room.

Practice your story

So what impression do you want them to have of you? Practice a one- or two-line statement that describes you and your story (perhaps explaining your presence) and make sure that's the one you deliver when asked – avoiding my usual trick of hiding behind self-deprecation. This can include making self-sabotaging declarations – a classic trait of mine in which I state that 'oh, I'm a nobody' or 'I'm the boring one you won't want to talk to', which usually results in me proving myself right.

Yet you don't need to push yourself forward. The aim is to build your confidence, not win a major contract or job offer. So – with your story prepared (just in case) – focus on enjoying the event and improving your people skills.

Watch your body language

As the NLPers will tell you, our body language is giving strong signals the entire time, so make sure this, too, is geared towards projecting confidence rather than timidity. Shoulders back, spine straight, head up, hands unclenched, arms unfolded – that sort of thing. Develop strong eye contact – not least because poor eye contact projects timidity more clearly than any other signal. Practice your smile so it at least looks genuine and also try to dress well. The wrong clothes can kill confidence almost instantly while a natty suit and sharp haircut can help you positively radiate.

Indeed, in terms of dress, a good gauge is to adopt the norms of the room. While outrageous clothes may get you noticed, they're for those that have the chutzpah to pull it off. For the shy, too strong a dress statement could undermine, rather than support, your confidence.

Avoid props
Take care when it comes to Dutch courage. Booze is an easy way to make yourself more confident but it has rapidly-diminishing returns with respect to your effectiveness. If you feel a glass of wine is required to 'oil the wheels' – fine. If you feel two or three are necessary, it may be worth noting whether your intake is ahead of others. Since I gave up drinking, my awareness of drinking habits at social events has increased: noticing both those that go to events and drink heavily – usually repeating themselves, finding unfunny jokes hilarious, becoming too tactile, rambling on incessantly and even slurring their words and looking unsteady – and those that don't – including nearly all those important people you may want to impress.

What's Stopping You Being More Confident? *Timidity is a common form of social panic, potentially the result of brain chemical imbalances. Yet it can be overcome through a mental realignment that includes strong preparation, being curious and developing good small talk.*

13

DEVELOPING CONFIDENCE AT WORK

With the traits for confidence understood, a plan hatched for our achievements and the limits of shyness or timidity side-stepped, confidence can become little more than the need to maintain progress. This is a great result, yet hurdles remain – not least at work and especially with respect to those we work with.

So what can we do to support our workplace confidence? We can change our attitude, that's what. We need to step through the looking-glass and observe the impact we have on those we work with – losing that typical but disabling trait of the under-confident: our obsession with the impact others have on us. This one change can make a fantastic difference to our effectiveness at work because it immediately empowers us. Suddenly, we're in charge of our own destiny because it's what *we* do that matters, rather than what *others* do to us. In fact, this is even true with respect to our seniors.

Certainly, becoming aware of our power as an individual in the workplace is a giant leap forward for the under-confident, as long as we then execute that power effectively. Use our power clumsily and we'll immediately build resistance from others. Deftly manipulate our power, meanwhile, and we'll be well on our way.

Of course, many people will have read the above passages and concluded they are powerless, making any manipulation of power a void concept. Yet such feelings simply prove the point that the under-confident waste their working lives obsessing about the impact others have on them (which, indeed, hands others the power), rather than noticing the impact they have on others. Watch carefully – and observe closely the impact *you* have – and the power of *your* position will become apparent. The only exceptions to this will be if your position is redundant, in which case your elevated view should reveal this and make finding a more useful role an urgent requirement.

What you can do

Having noticed your power – even if just the dependencies your role generates – you need to build upon it: endowing your position with further faculty and building your self-efficacy over time. Of course, this requires grace and tact – as ever. And it requires the division of your tactics into two realms: those that focus on what *you* can do to improve *your* position (the subject of this chapter), and those that focus on what *you* can do when dealing with *others* to the same end (the subject of Chapter 14).

Bolstering your own power

As stated, many under-confident people feel powerless, especially at work. But they needn't. Bolstering our power in the workplace is – to a major extent – in our own hands. Many strategies, tactics and attitudes can be adopted without any input from others. Here are some:

1. Assume you're not being exploited
Too many people regard the workplace environment as one in which they're exploited. That somehow the owners are stealing their time, their endeavour, their creativity. And once such an attitude is embedded it's hard to shift. Like conspiracy theorists, we spend our time looking for evidence to prove our theory – and we usually find it (as, indeed, do the conspiracy theorists).

But are we *really* being exploited? Forced to work the lord's land for no payment, the serfs of medieval Europe were certainly exploited, as were the indentured labourers of the eighteenth century: chained in servitude to pay off their passage to the New World. And the small children of poorer countries today, kept out of school to shell nuts for supermarkets – they're most definitely exploited. But are you – just because someone somewhere has managed to negotiate slightly better terms for doing a similar job (you think)?

Feelings of being conned are corrosive in the extreme because they spiral you down rather than build you up. They're a mental ball and chain that prevent you doing your job well – contributing instead to your (self-designated) lowly status. And it's just one view, which you can change by seeing your job – any job – as a stairway to a better place. The best mental realignment I can think of is to *always* consider yourself 'work-in-progress'. So rather than view your job as a drudge – and your role as unappreciated by others – you should adopt Dweck's growth mindset and see it as an apprenticeship for the next level.

Far from theft, your job is a gift: teaching you competence (and therefore self-efficacy) in a particular area. And if you've achieved all the competence the post can offer: well, maybe that's a signal to move on up. That said, seniors may have spotted your negative attitude and concluded that you're incapable (or unworthy) of advancement.

2. Be conscientious

Being conscientious is simply a follow-on from quashing those convictions of exploitation. But it's a vital one for your confidence. Deep inside you know when you're doing your best, and when you're slacking. Yet, again, slacking (perhaps because you feel exploited) is a one-way street in the wrong direction. It's de-energizing in the extreme: lowering your motivation, undermining your well-being and sapping your confidence. So do the opposite: work hard.

'Confidence comes as a direct result, not of success, but of effort,' says Ilise Benun (2006), by which she means that working hard gets the mind whirring and the adrenaline flowing. It's energizing and empowering. It cheers us up through feelings of achievement, which – of course – support our confidence.

Indeed, conscientiousness is so important for our confidence that Ros Taylor devotes a whole chapter to it in *Confidence at Work* (2011), although she states that being conscientious is more than simply working hard – it's working towards a vision of what we want to achieve. As we did with our own plans for achievement, she asks us to develop a mission statement for our work, perhaps covering the next few months. It should be specific, action-oriented, stretching and pleasing to say.

And once we have a mission statement – perhaps to 'work hard and get noticed' – we need to knuckle down and get on with it. We should stop complaining, stop erecting barriers and stop looking for excuses because such behaviours reinforce our under-confidence.

3. Have a plan (but slow it down)

Of course, Ros Taylor's mission statement points us in the right direction and should, hopefully, motivate us to achieve. Yet we need to think well beyond six months. As stated, we need detailed plans that take care of the next five or even 10 years. Of course, under-confident people can struggle to generate long-term plans they fully believe in.

So, if you're still struggling, here's a shortcut . . .

A key aspect of planning is to link your desired future to your present circumstances, offering a route between the two. If you can decide on your desired destination, therefore, you can then join the dots through a series of stages, each getting you closer to your goal and each motivating you to get the most from your current position (while keeping an eye out for opportunities to advance).

For instance, if you're an office cleaner now and want to become an actor in five years (and maybe a TV star in 10), how can you join the dots?

- *Dot/year one:* Swap office cleaning for theatre cleaning.
- *Dot/year two:* You've become chief cleaner, although you're meanwhile looking to expand your role. You've got to know the theatre and stated your intentions (see Chapter 14), as well as joined the theatre's amateur dramatics club.
- *Dot/year three:* You've moved to backstage operations (now seen and heard by the actors and directors), and become a leading light in the drama club.
- *Dot/year four: Yikes!* You're understudying a key role, having to rehearse with the actors. And you're now in charge of back-stage ops. Oh, and a small role's come up in the Christmas pantomime.
- *Dot/year five:* You've won an important role in a new production!

Given this trajectory, the next five dots to TV stardom should be a doddle. And if you're reading the above and thinking 'cleaner to TV star: yeah right', it's worth noting that I became a journalist by first selling classified advertisements for a national broadsheet, winning an editorial position by concocting articles on the environment and lobbying the editors for inclusion.

Therefore, such a route is not only doable (because your only need is to get to the next stage) it also offers a realistic timeframe, which should decrease frustrations and increase patience (though some frustration and a little impatience are beneficial traits for progression).

4. Don't undermine yourself

Self-sabotage is a common trait in the under-confident. We often communicate our poor confidence to those around us – forcing them to adopt the negative view we hold of ourselves. This can be via the innocent-seeming cloak of modesty or self-deprecation, which – nonetheless – has the same aim: to deliberately lower other's expectations of us. In reality, however, we're pleading for mercy: communicating the fact we pose no threat in the hope of avoiding attack.

Watch any herd or pack of animals on a farm or roaming the savannah and you'll see the same power games being played out. The strong: posturing – alive to, and facing down, threats. The weak: cowering – avoiding the attention of the silverback or stallion for fear of attack. It's no different in the workplace. The strong and ambitious are beating their chest while those lacking confidence communicate their weakness in the hope of being left alone.

Yet, while a natural animalistic response, we're undermining our progress and compounding our poor confidence. We're not dumb animals. We're sophisticated humans in a modern place of employment – meaning we *can* develop a more effective response.

We just need to be clever: not talking ourselves down, but avoiding overly talking ourselves up (equally a trait of the insecure). We have both long-term and medium-term plans, as well as immediate tactics to execute. And we simply need to follow them to the best of our abilities. Over time, we'll be noticed, and even if we're not – well, we're still be in a better place mentally. Remember, achievements are achievements because they get us closer to our goals and build our self-efficacy – not because some senior has given us a pathetic pat on the back. As stated, the recognition of our achievements is important, but making approval our *only* focus is asking to waste our lives trying to please others.

As for dealing with the rutting stag? Why not seek win:win outcomes in which you're helping them achieve *their* goals? It'll reduce tensions, build alliances and smooth your path towards achievement – all without having to lock antlers in feuds that, in the office environment, tend to damage everyone involved.

5. Understand your company
Knowing the company or organization you work for is vital. No, I mean *really* knowing it:

- *Who runs your organization?* Not just the names of the chairman, CEO and board of directors but the entire board and even the heads of departments. And their backgrounds as well. Where have they all come from, what projects do they champion, what's their philosophy? Every morsel of information will make you a more effective operator at work – increasing your confidence. It'll also help you spot opportunities and – just as importantly – prevent you wasting time on work that's going nowhere. Such information is usually publicly-available or easily discovered (often by listening to those around you).

- *What about your sector?* Every industry sector is a 'vertical universe' – a narrow world with its own history, geography and politics. There are champions and challengers, risers and fallers, celebrities and heroes: these days all accessible via the click of a mouse. There's no excuse for not knowing the latest innovations, legal rulings, mergers or deals, or even just gossip. Your sector's story is written and available, and should be consumed ravenously by those wanting confidence in the workplace – not least because it'll put you eye-to-eye with the seniors. Sure, the phrase 'information is power' is a cliché. But it's also true.

- *And don't forget the technicalities.* Of course, it's not just the players and gossip that matter, it's what your organization actually does. You need to get under the bonnet and take an interest, not least because it may reveal your total disregard for the sector you're in. Certainly, I find this at Moorgate with our new graduates. Finance fascinates me because, after writing about it as a journalist, I realized the power of finance as a means for generating social benefits (a message lost since the 2008 crisis). But finance was a taste I had to acquire – and there are those we take on who simply cannot acquire it, which will always undermine their confidence. Invariably, I say to the financially disinterested that they must find what interests them to the point they'll want to soak up the technicalities. Some have left for health sector PR, others for consumer branding: a great result – as long as their new world fascinates them enough for them to love the nuts and bolts.

6. Get yourself known

To get yourself known, you don't have to march upstairs and intro-duce yourself to all the seniors on your first day (although it's an effective gambit if you can muster the courage). Just put yourself about – introduce yourself to unknown faces (using the tactics discussed for social events). This doesn't have to be forced: it's simply being friendly and open to meeting people. Nearly all organ-izations are networks of people, and most people are keen to know others around the building (with those that aren't again discounting themselves as unimportant). It's also a great use of all that informa-tion we've gathered – turning names into faces and departments into people.

And if we get in the lift with the boss? Well we can ask them about the Johnson bid, or the Jeffries Ruling, or the Brighton con-ference they're speaking at – anything that gets them talking and indicates your interest in the organization's welfare.

That said, we should also be nice to receptionists, PAs, office managers and even security guards. These people understand the geo-politics of an organization at the most intimate level. They know where the (metaphorical) landmines are located, as well as the secret tunnels and ladders for advancement. Many are gatekeep-ers of one sort or another, most have the ear of at least one senior and they all make better friends than enemies.

7. Avoid affected uselessness

Demarcation is a drag on self-efficacy. Strict boundaries with respect to your job can prevent you developing competences and expanding your horizons, especially if you bump up against those feeling guarded about their role. Yet too often we demarcate our-selves – becoming reluctant or even refusing to go beyond our brief because of some perceived boundary. This is especially the case with jobs we feel are beneath us, perhaps involving our workstation functionality. Too often our response is to throw up our hands and assume someone else will change the toner, load the printer, work out why our email has stopped working, etc.

Yet in each case we're signalling our uselessness to those we work with. Sure, we may actually be ignorant of some technicality. But there's the open response, in which we seek help in order to acquire the skill. And there's the closed response, in which we surrender our competence by mentally crossing our arms and refusing to work until some minion has put it right. In reality, this is no more than a sulk: a mental refusal, even if delivered – as it sometimes is – as a beguiling or even flirtatious affectation.

As for making the tea or buying the biscuits or answering the phone or any one of the other functions that make workplace environments bearable – be the person that leads rather than follows. Nothing makes a better impression on those around you than showing public willingness for executing the niceties. In fact – as with being publicly polite – it's such a cheap and easy way to make a strong impression I'm amazed people aren't falling over themselves to answer the phone or make each other tea.

8. Enjoy your job
Look around an office and those that enjoy their job stand out. They're engaged, positive, forthcoming, optimistic, open to suggestion, happy to contribute, proactive and mostly cheerful. They also ooze self-efficacy (a result of their happy employment). Yet those that don't enjoy their job are equally obvious. They are distracted, guarded, defensive, negative, pessimistic, reactive and mostly grumpy. Scratch the surface, and most also harbour deep insecurities regarding their competence – often masked through constantly blaming others for every negative event, or even what they perceive as the structural uselessness of their organization.

Being on the wrong side of this equation is miserable, corrosive and self-destructive. It renders you powerless and destroys your confidence. In my view, it's worth risking ruin and starvation to avoid, although such extremes are not normally necessary. Mostly, we just need to research what interests us, create a plan for our future and a strategy for our actions. And then we need to get on and find a workplace that motivates us.

What's Stopping You Being More Confident? *Confidence at work requires a change in attitude to one where your concern is the impact you have on others (rather than the impact they have on you). Yet you must expand your power through conscientiousness and by avoiding self-sabotage. You must also understand your work environment and get yourself known.*

14

WORKING WITH OTHERS

So there's a lot we can do to increase our power in the workplace without any input from anyone else. Yet there's also a lot we cannot do. Others matter: whether senior or junior, colleagues or customers, or whether a direct report or someone only tangentially relevant to our role.

Developing people skills is therefore important if we're to increase our confidence at work. In fact – given that it's other people that are mostly responsible for our under-confidence – dealing with others is the absolute apocalypse of our endeavours. Get this right and we're well on our way. That said, if we fail here we remain condemned to the purgatory of under-confidence.

Again, planning and strategizing are important – but these have been previously tackled. It's the daily tactics that matter now – the small stuff that, nonetheless, chips away at our confidence. Here are my thoughts on developing people skills in the workplace: based on a lifetime of getting it (mostly) wrong.

1. Learn to say no

This is a favourite of the self-help universe. Many people have their confidence attacked and their self-esteem sapped by an inability to say no, they say – making this a vital requisite for confidence-seekers. Ilise Benun's (2006) view is typical of what seems to be a consensus:

'The ability to say 'no' is crucial to success in business,' she says. 'It plays a role in managing, setting up realistic expectations, establishing trust and being a professional.'

Of course I agree with this. But I'm also concerned that we remain strategic – keeping our long-term objectives in mind. An abrupt refusal may harm our standing and damage, rather than build, our confidence. We should perhaps examine why we want to say no. Are we too busy? Well, we can point to all our outstanding tasks, and their deadlines, and politely suggest a need to prioritize. Or is it because we feel the job is beneath us? Fine, but then whose job is it? Perhaps we can visibly (i.e. noticeably) delegate the task to them, which should help build our competence at delegation (see below) as well as communicate confidence to those around us (although beware 'affected uselessness').

Or is it that we feel the person asking lacks respect, or is leveraging off our insecurities to exploit us (a likely scenario given our poor confidence)? In this case delicacy is required. Maybe we should deliver on the task but add a polite message (at the point of delivery) that this went beyond the call of duty and, while happy to do this as a favour – this once – it's not something we can be expected to do repeatedly without complaint. Especially if the task is executed with panache – and the message is delivered well – we'll have built rather than undermined our confidence.

2. State your intentions

Unfortunately, we are judged on our actions rather than our intentions. And the actions of the under-confident often communicate meekness. We can act as if we lack ambition. As if we deserve nothing more than to be overlooked or even disrespected. Certainly, we can look and sound powerless and radiate weakness: no wonder our poor confidence is so often confirmed by the actions of others.

Reversing this requires a bold and powerful statement of our intentions. Perhaps we should source a meeting with our seniors and articulate our purpose: '*This* is my ambition within the organization.' Of course, we'll have to explain our previous poor showing as well as what the 'new me' aims to achieve. Yes, the 'old me' sent the wrong signals we can say. But they're no longer valid.

This tells them straight: please judge me afresh. It also sets a benchmark for us to adhere to – a new standard by which we can judge ourselves, and expect to be judged by others. Yet we cannot do this and then continue to act as the meek, moaning, and seemingly exploited person of old. We have to change. But it means that the change has been stated and will, hopefully, be noticed. And if it isn't? Then we have the strongest signal yet we may be in an organization harmful to our long-term confidence, meaning we should stay positive but plan our exit.

3. Learn to delegate

Ken Blanchard became famous for writing the *One Minute Manager* (1981) in which he extolled the virtues of delegation – true delegation in which, as the delegator, we simply agree a vision regarding the result of a particular task or project and then completely back off: giving them the autonomy to execute their own achievement. They may make mistakes, but they'll learn from them, whereas those we instruct every step of the way learn nothing more than an ability to carry out detailed instructions.

It's important to remember that Blanchard wasn't simply writing for managers trying to instruct juniors. His philosophy extends to anyone working in an environment that may involve one person having to offload tasks to someone else, which is a highly problematic area for the under-confident. While feeling exploited, the under-confident can also become defensive when asked to pass on part of their role: perhaps to a new junior or maybe a colleague

reporting to the same manager. We may receive the request to delegate as a threat – an attempt to strip us of even this low level of
authority or autonomy.

Yet we should see it as the opposite. It's a chance to increase
our power – either by recruiting others to our sphere of influence
or by releasing us from a mindless task that we probably previously judged exploitative. So delegation is something that *must* be
embraced, although good delegation is an acquired skill – involving
(according to Blanchard) less, rather than more, instruction.

But it also requires confidence. After all, those we delegate to
could be more skilled, which may undermine our credibility. So we
need to have faith that, by delegating, we're giving ourselves the
space to grow – rather than handing over a small part of our
pathetic empire. We're recruiting people to our cause, not losing
functionality from our role: admittedly a difficult mental assumption for the under-confident because it involves the issue of trust
(as previously discussed in Part Two).

4. Overcome hesitation

Key moments decide our progress: not just during the stress of
Sullivan's *clutch* but in the instant opportunities that may appear
from nowhere and disappear almost as fast. Perhaps the CEO has
addressed us out of the blue, or we meet the boss of our ideal
company at an event.

'Life all comes down to a few moments: this is one of them,'
said Bud Fox (Charlie Sheen) before his life-changing meeting with
Gordon Gekko (Michael Douglas) in the 1987 movie *Wall Street*.
So we need to make them count.

Here are my tips for doing so:

* *Prepare an 'elevator pitch'*. This is entrepreneur-speak for those
  key moments – perhaps when you share a lift with the boss –
  that offer you literally seconds to impart your business idea to

the one person that could make all the difference. Thinking on the spot at such a time is almost impossible, so you need a prepared line: 'Hi, Mr Walsh, I'm Jenny. I work in accounts but I'm focused on moving to sales as soon as I can.' Resist adding 'can you help?' They'll get your drift, and backing them into a corner will not improve your chances. You just need to state your intentions, use positive language and smile. That said, you should also thank your previous commitment to *always* dress professionally in the office, giving out strong signals that support your ambitions.

- *Accept imperfect circumstances.* A key moment came for me when working in a production job for a finance-focused magazine. I wanted an editorial role and said as much to the editor when we coincidentally shared a taxi to an office function. I've done a good job on production, I said (in fact the conversation had started with her complimenting my skills and diligence), and I can also prove my worth on the editorial side if given the chance. She was impressed by the fact I was willing to state my ambition frankly – as well as do so in a taxi shared by another member of staff. Of course, I'd rather the third passenger hadn't been there to witness my cringe-worthy pitch. But there she sat – and I wasn't going to let the opportunity pass.

- *State your intentions.* Important people have a lot on their mind, so don't mince your words. Most are good at picking up the nuances (it's their job) and don't need to be asked directly for help. But most also appreciate plain speaking rather than cryptic prose because their time is precious and your ability to articulate well says a lot about you. And those that don't appreciate such boldness? Well that says a lot about them.

- *Regret action not inaction.* Even if your pitch falls flat, even if it's embarrassing, even if it ends up as a locker room tale in which you are noisily mocked – so what? As former England football manager Terry Venables once said: 'Don't regret not doing something, regret doing it' – a worthy mantra for the under-confident to adopt.

5. Learn to persuade

Of course, Terry Venables had a trait all successful people possess: he could persuade. He could charm the pants off anyone he met, not least because he oozed chutzpah. That said, even those less blessed with the sprinkled stardust of natural persuasiveness can develop their skills in this respect.

'Good persuasion . . . involves understanding the true needs and desires of the person you are persuading, understanding his or her criteria for action, and finally presenting information in a way that is congruent with his or her indicated desires,' writes Dave Lakhani in *Persuasion: The Art of Getting What You Want* (2005).

Lakhani is quick to point out that persuasion is not manipulation because there's no deception. The persuader is simply trying to point out common interests, potentially fostering long-term and mutually beneficial relationships. This makes persuasion similar to Stephen Covey's habit of 'synergizing' (of looking for commonalities with everyone we meet – another effective trait of the confident), although we must remember that, ultimately, we're trying to move people towards our needs.

Lakhani points out the key traits of the persuaders (with some thoughts of my own):

- *A good voice.* This is more than a booming and strident tone. It means enunciating words well, maintaining eye contact and having positive body language. Ultimately, persuaders are asking to be followed – so you must sound like you know where you're going.
- *A strong network.* Persuaders can nearly always name a connection or person that can bridge the gap between you and them. This increases the persuader's integrity and credibility – making them the missing link you've been waiting years to meet.
- *A good story.* Persuaders know their story and can tell it convincingly. Lakhani points to three story requirements: your biography (how you got here); your company (or position/

department if internal); and your proposition to that individual. Each must be compelling.

- *Authority.* This cannot be faked. You need to establish your area of expertise, study hard, develop a perspective (or opinion), and believe in it. Only those that believe in what they say can hope to persuade others.
- *Belief alignment.* Persuaders try and first understand the beliefs of those they seek to persuade, and then try and align themselves as closely as possible with those beliefs. If your aim is to move their beliefs, start with the elements that overlap, slowly trying to expand them to encompass your view. Starting in the deep blue water between your positions – and assuming your power of persuasion is enough – will almost certainly fail.

Other Lakhani techniques include the 'gift to receive', in which we offer something first in order to encourage reciprocity (a favourite trick of the cheese counter in delis); offering inconsequential steps towards your desired result (what I call the 'A-to-Z-via-B', in which we focus only on getting others to the seemingly innocuous B); and 'social matching', in which we show that similar people have been previously persuaded and benefited.

6. Give rather than seek compliments

Everyone enjoys a compliment. But the under-confident can obsess about them – making compliments their only quest, which renders them powerless. Despite the empowering feeling a compliment offers, therefore, we must remember that the recipient is soaking up the power of the giver, which increases our dependence on them.

Gaining confidence is not about receiving compliments, therefore, it's about giving them. Certainly the giver is more important than the receiver, although – that said – handing out compliments is probably the cheapest form of effective empowerment available, so we should actively adopt it.

Of course, many people view compliments as cheesy or smarmy: sleazy even. So we have to become adept at giving them – perhaps making indirect comments such as 'what a fantastic cake' or 'what amazing creativity', rather than the more direct 'Sandra, you're *sooo* brilliant at cake making'. That said, watch Sandra's reaction to the full-on adulation and the power of the compliment will become apparent.

7. Don't sweat the boss

Ask the under-confident to name the one person chaining them to their lowly outlook and the chances are it'll be their boss. Indeed, strong progress elsewhere can be negated swiftly by our seniors, who can end up obsessing us and therefore destroying any crumbs of confidence we may be accumulating.

To gain confidence, therefore, we *must* tackle our boss. But care is required. Battle against your boss and you may be David beating Goliath, the Boers outsmarting the British Empire or the Viet Cong defeating the Americans. More likely, however, you'll be one of the thousands of forgotten heroes that have taken on a stronger foe and lost, which will be a disaster for your confidence.

So do the opposite. Rather than detest your boss, work with them. In his charming 1998 book *Don't Sweat the Small Stuff at Work*, Dr Richard Carlson offers the following titbits for dealing with our 'dear leaders' (with some thoughts of my own):

- *'Don't sweat the demanding boss.'* There are two ways of dealing with the demanding boss, Carlson states. We can complain about them (perhaps behind their backs) or we can try and see through their impact on us. He asks us to note that demanding people tend to be so with everyone, so we shouldn't take it personally. He also states that they, most likely, have no hidden motives, so don't assume any. Many, he states, are stuck in the role of being demanding, which means that – like the personal trainer pushing you harder – the demanding boss may be the very person willing *you* to achieve more. Even if that's doubtful, it's certainly a healthier view when trying to cope with their demands.

- *'Let go of battles that cannot be won.'* As stated, battling against the boss is usually a one-way ticket to defeat. They may be wrong, and heading for certain humiliation. But Carlson warns against fighting too hard to prevent it. Having stated your view there are occasions when we must remember that it's the bosses reputation on the line, not ours. So they have to pick their own path. If they were right, and you were supportive (but wrong) they'll forgive you (and enjoy their victory). If they were wrong, and you pointed out their error (but remained onside) – well, maybe next time they'll listen.

- *'Before becoming defensive, take note of what is being said.'* I wish I'd known this one when I was a journalist or banker. If my former seniors were asked to describe me in one word, my guess is the word 'defensive' would crop up time and time again. For the defensive, even constructive criticism requires a knee-jerk and instantaneous reaction. Of course, many's the time when – with time and emotion elapsed – I realized their words made perfect sense. So why was I so incapable of hearing this truth earlier? In fact, my boss was saying something sensible probably 90 percent of the time – and having to battle against my defensive shield in order to get through. And the 10 percent of times they were being a jerk? Well, clear the fog of defensiveness and their nonsense becomes obvious.

- *'Remember to appreciate the people you work with.'* Yes, this is even true of the boss, although Carlson's main focus is on colleagues and even the office cleaner. But my view is that all the tactics we've learnt regarding dealing with people – about giving compliments and being nice – also apply to our seniors. Certainly, if one of my juniors pays me a compliment I appreciate it enormously. After all, I'm the one cutting through the jungle – it's my head above the parapet. And their view of me is all important, although it must be genuine. Sure, their colleagues may consider it 'brown-nosing' – a horrible expression reserved for the bitter and insecure, in my opinion. But, if delivered well (and perhaps indirectly), it will increase your standing no-end.

8. Handle challenging people with elegance

If only our boss was the only difficult person in the workplace. But he/she isn't. Difficult people exist in every office – many, the under-confident jobsworths whose fate we're so desperate to avoid.

According to conflict specialist Muriel Solomon in *Working with Difficult People* (2002), office antagonists come in various guises, each requiring a different strategic response (as ever, with some thoughts of my own):

- *Hostile people.* Burdened with personal problems, the hostile are usually angry and depressed. They'll look hard for your weak points and use those as their focus for attack. According to Solomon we should avoid their trap by staying cool. They want to rattle you, so don't let them push your buttons. Stay calm, and they look the insecure ones, not you.

- *Pushy people.* Arrogant colleagues want to jam their ideas down your throat, so don't let them. Most are insecure and want to be liked – the classic realm of the bully. We simply need to realize they're this way with everyone, and remain open-minded and accessible despite their behaviour. Don't face down their pushiness or confront it directly: simply side-step it. If they cannot recruit you, you'll be communicating your confidence – making you more and more desirable as an ally. Enjoy the power!

- *Deceitful people.* Liars cheat and distort the facts. They can be hypocritical: nice to your face and horrible behind your back. Yet, again, they're communicating their insecurities. We need to rise above them, making sure they don't drag us down to their level. And if our boss is one? Always remain professional when with them and try and get their commitments in writing. Also, take comfort from the fact their deceit is nothing personal – it's just their under-confidence making them act this way.

- *Shrewd people.* While deceitful people are insecure, the shrewd are usually highly-confident – and are using your insecurities to get what they want. Notice how they behave, perhaps by putting you under direct pressure to do something and feigning surprise when you resist. They may know what you want and offer it as a reward, although it may be a myth. Fine, so why not turn the tables and be as direct in return? Question their games – and notice when they change tack (or become hostile because you've revealed their subterfuge). But be careful: shrewd people make tough opponents for the under-confident.

- *Rude people.* Meanwhile, the rude are easy to deal with. Even if they're hitting out at your genuine incompetence, their approach has given you your best defence. There are few modern workplaces where open rudeness or disrespect is acceptable. Indeed, in many western countries it's illegal. So make it clear that their insults are beyond the pale. Establish clear boundaries of acceptable behaviour and politely ask them not to cross the line. That said, many will calm down and apologize, which you should accept gracefully – perhaps by also apologizing, no matter what the circumstances. Indeed, you've won your victory, so being magnanimous will help build alliances while stubbornness will only convert it into a defeat.

- *Egotistical people.* Conceited people are grandstanders, says Solomon. They are self-centred and want to show off. Yet they occupy a self-contained universe, which rarely has any direct impact on you (though may still grate). That said, know-it-all colleagues or subordinates can be particularly aggravating, which requires us to develop some tactics for dealing with them. Ask penetrating questions that demand quantifiable answers. And don't take what they say as gospel – the egotistic are prone to exaggerate. Yet remain objective. And remember that most egotists are insecure at heart, no matter how well they hide it. So the wry smile may be a better tactic than the full-frontal putdown (and the occasional indulgence of their ego is even better).

- *Procrastinating people.* More self-esteem issues to deal with – this time from those incapable of making decisions. Yet, while frustrating, such insecurities in others represent an opportunity for us – not to beat them but to recognize their fears and help. By aligning with their concerns you can become the trusted adviser, which – if to a senior – is one of the most important positions within any organization. As for juniors, we can teach them what we've learnt about breaking projects down into doable action points – helping build confidence around us (which should also help our own).

- *Critical people.* Some people are incapable of expressing satisfaction – picking on the tiniest element in order to find something to criticize. If your boss does this, it can be soul-destroying in the extreme, although a direct confrontation is (as always) worth avoiding. Of course, we should take note of the criticism while not letting it undermine our confidence – being aware that our horizons go well beyond their immediate displeasure. That said, constantly critical people are depressing, so we cannot be entirely passive if we're to prevent them knocking our confidence. One tactic I've developed is to offer the ironic riposte. While not over-playing it (and while accepting genuine feedback) the 'thank you for your positivity' statement can leave them wondering, and you smiling, and any damage to your confidence neutered.

With all challenging people we should aim to adopt the motto of the now famous World War Two poster: 'Keep calm and carry on'. If you can hold your nerve (as well as your tongue) and continue to communicate, no matter what the aggravation, you should be able to develop elegance when dealing with people. And this will build your confidence, which is a fantastic result for previously under-confident people.

> **What's Stopping You Being More Confident?** *Developing people skills is crucial for confidence. Small tactics can be effective, such as stating your intentions, learning to delegate, overcoming hesitation and mastering persuasion. But you should also learn to handle the boss and deal with challenging people elegantly.*

15

DATING

One area too frequently ignored by confidence gurus concerns our romantic interests. Even when not ignored, this is a subject often tackled through generalities that, while helpful, fail to reach the nub of our needs. I can't blame them, of course, because this is a controversial area in which we can be accused of gender stereotyping and even of being sexist. My desire to tackle this subject head-on should, therefore, contain a health warning: reading on may cause offence.

Poor confidence is gender-specific

Of course, there's much overlap with respect to the two genders when it comes to romance and dating. But the overlap is least apparent when dealing with what drives poor confidence in this area. Men and women tend to be under-confident about different things, based (if I may be so bold) on the different roles assigned to us by nature. So, while making no judgements on the appropriateness of such roles – or how outdated they can seem – my focus here is on being useful to both genders.

This means honestly tackling where I think under-confident men have most problems, which is in meeting women and succeeding in those early encounters. And where I think most under-confident women have difficulty, which is in converting those early but brief encounters into a fulfilling and sustainable relationship.

I could have assumed no difference in outlook or need and – like the majority of self-help writers before me – left readers to pick their own gender differences from such neutered tips as 'keep it light' and 'be on time'. Yet I think this dishonest. Certainly, I found such advice of little use to me when watching male peers succeed in attracting women while I stood on the sidelines, frustrated that my acute lack of confidence was preventing me from even talking to the opposite sex.

Like many men, my poor romantic or sexual confidence when young was underlined by feeling unattractive: that I lacked some ingredient vital for captivating women. In my case this was height. I'm 5'8", while my successful male peers all seemed to be taller, which made them immediately more confident with women.

This is hardly uncommon. Instant judgements of attractiveness are made by both sexes: meaning that, if we're in some way different from the stereotypical image of beauty – by being short or fat or gangly or facially unattractive (whether real or imagined) – we're likely to lack confidence at those crucial moments when first being evaluated by the opposite sex.

Fear of rejection and humiliation

For men this is particularly painful. Even today, it's the male of the species that's usually required to make the initial moves in those vital early exchanges when meeting prospective romantic partners: making any loss of confidence at this point all the more agonizing. Men have to put themselves up for rejection and humiliation, something the short or fat or 'ugly' guy is convinced is coming: making poor confidence all but inevitable.

No wonder, also, that so many opt out of the game – becoming wallflowers or even avoiding social situations. Indeed, agony aunt columns are full of the sorry tales of the self-rejected male. One I read in a discarded tabloid newspaper on the underground went something like this:

'I'm 19 and 5'6" and feel my height has become a major disadvantage in my social life. While my friends are out clubbing and chatting to girls, I've lost confidence and now avoid social situations because I worry girls will reject me or even laugh at me.'

My heart went out to this young lad, although my empathy turned to anger upon reading the agony aunt's reply. She wrote that, at 19, he could still grow. Meanwhile, she recommended counselling to explore why his height was causing him to lose confidence.

That was it! This was a woefully inadequate response, in my opinion – in fact, little more than a dismissal, as if she too found under-confident short guys a bit of a pain. I felt I could do better and posted an answer on my blog – a posting that, to this day, has received more positive attention than any other. I offered 10 points of advice that, although focused on height, can – with little adjustment – play equally well with other physical traits that disable male confidence at the very point it's most needed.

Here's my version – adjusted to include all males struggling with confidence on the dating scene:

1. First the bad news. You may grow (or otherwise change physically) but you may not. In fact, my guess is that your loss of confidence is a natural response to this realization: something you have to absorb while also noting that attracting the opposite sex has become the central preoccupation of your peer group. Yet facing your demons is a positive. Denial or fantasizing, meanwhile, would be a ridiculous response.

2. Does it matter? Yes, it does. There's no denying it, physical beauty is important when trying to attract females and, for men, height is a key part of the package (as is physique and facial beauty). So your pool of available females is reduced. Yet, over time, this in-built disadvantage will disappear.

3. At 19, feeling physically unattractive to women is indeed agony. Yet women tend to most admire male confidence. It's just that height or beauty give men strong confidence. That

said, physical attributes don't have a monopoly on bolstering male confidence. As we have seen, achievement has the same effect. And, at 19, you have your entire adulthood to win confidence through achievement.

4. Time changes your physical appearance. At 19 I was both short and thin. Yet by 30 I'd filled out, improving my confidence but also meaning I had to make efforts to stay trim, something that further boosted my confidence. And as my body confidence grew I noticed those earlier 'Kings of the Nightclub' starting to age: perhaps becoming overweight or losing their hair (which is no respecter of height or looks). I'm not being competitive here, just stating that confidence can be gained with your physical appearance not only at any stage but also from your own efforts. And if you lack confidence now – perhaps because you feel unattractive – you therefore owe it to yourself to make the effort.

5. That said, in just a few years from now your physical appearance (although always a factor) will decline in significance. At your age, few people are settling into long-term relationships so the whole game feels like an episode of *90210* or *Hollyoaks*. Yet this phase is short-lived and, soon enough, flings start converting into longer-term relationships that require a different set of attributes. Honesty, commitment, humour, tolerance: all are traits required for successful long-term relationships. Meanwhile, the good-looking tall guy may have developed alternative traits – including arrogance, vanity and selfishness – that become increasingly ugly to women seeking a life partner (even if those traits seemed initially attractive).

6. Yet the above benefits are to come. What advice can help you while still 19? First is the fact you may be socializing in the wrong place. At your age I lived in Essex – land of the glamour nightspots and shallow vanities. My confidence was rock bottom. Once at university in Manchester, however, the whole scene changed to one where I was judged on my personality rather than my appearance. My height insecurities

disappeared, not least because the very trait seen as unattractive in Essex – my desire for meaningful conversation – became
appreciated.

7. And it may also be worth remembering that the whole night-
    club scenario – boy approaches girl and tries to chat her up
    – is a total pain for all but the shallowest female. Worthy
    partners will not appreciate the nightclub pick-up because
    they'll assume you're just another jerk playing the numbers
    game. So don't be that jerk. Instead, seek a social life
    where some form of verbal inter-action is at least possible.
    Tennis clubs are a favourite, as are art gallery openings
    and evening talks (perhaps at museums). What's more, nearly
    all are swamped with nice and intelligent women avoiding
    those Lothario-infested nightclubs but still keen on meeting
    (intelligent) men.

8. Indeed, develop your personality. Clearly, your physical
    appearance makes you miserable. Yet the key thing to remem-
    ber is that it's your reactions that are unattractive – not you
    physically. Short guys are always getting the girl, as are geeky,
    'ugly' or fat guys: self-haters, sulkers and depressives, mean-
    while, will only attract others with the same insecurities.
    Along with confidence, most women absolutely love a cheeky
    smile and a joke, both of which are impossible while focused
    on the potential downside of your physical appearance.

9. Never wear or do anything to mask your physical appearance.
    For short guys this means high-heels or lifts, although I often
    judge outrageous piercings, facial tattoos or punk hairstyles
    as radical attempts at disguising often self-assessed ugliness.
    Even if initially successful, these will ultimately compound
    your insecurities. That said, just as the gym can add confi-
    dence, so can being well-dressed. I don't mean frontal-lobotomy
    designer crap. I mean clothes carefully selected to enhance
    your looks and confidence (it may be worth hiring a personal
    shopper or style consultant for an afternoon). Hair and

general grooming are also important – an area you may have neglected due to your poor confidence.

10. Finally, you may need to reframe your view of the jibes and insults you receive from both men and women. Just as you have about your physical appearance, nearly everyone has some insecurity that eats away at them even if they're good at hiding it. This is mostly revealed by put-downs of others or joy at another's misfortune. And we need to see them as such.

I once met a very confident short man and asked him if he was ever bothered by negative comments about his height. 'You mean from insecure tall men?' he said. 'That's just them revealing their inadequacies.' It took me years to realize the fundamental truth of this statement, but I now accept this as fact: if the only thing going for you is your height or looks, you knock the short or fat or 'ugly' guy in a desperate attempt to impose your warped view of hierarchy.

As for women that make nasty remarks or laugh? Well, they may have you down as a pest (which is unfair but understandable). If not – and especially if the put-down is aired for public appreciation – it's just them expressing their own insecurities, which says more about them than it does about you. That said – and in my experience – this is a rare occurrence (and one I've never experienced outside of the shallowest environs of my home county).

Avoid *The Rules*

So, men should avoid 'playing the game' when it comes to dating. Instead, they should look to reinforce their confidence with the opposite sex by developing their personality beyond the gladiatorial arena of the nightclub. But what about women – many of whom may be more concerned about attracting a reliable long-term partner? Well, in this case, women should avoid playing 'the rules'.

The Rules: Time-tested Secrets for Capturing the Heart of Mr Right (1995) by Ellen Fein and Sherrie Schneider is probably the most famous book ever written for single females on the dating scene and has probably done more to harm the advancement of women than anything since the invention of the scold's bridle.

I hate this book. Not because it made my life difficult as an amorous male on the New York and London dating circuits in the 1990s, but because – in my opinion – its appalling recommendations destroy the confidence of the very people it's trying to help: women seeking worthwhile relationships with half-decent men.

There are 35 'rules' in total, but a few will give you a taste:

- *Don't stare at men or talk too much.* This is not advice for travelling on public transport. They mean in a bar or at a social event. And by staring they mean *any* eye-to-eye contact with *any* man. Women should 'just smile at the room'. Meanwhile, any woman feeling chatty should also realize that garrulousness is apparently off-putting for potential male suitors, so forget finding commonality through conversation.
- *Don't call him and rarely return his calls.* While I agree it's important to not seem too keen (making the man work hard for your attentions), only a pest is likely to persist through such stark rejection signals as not returning his calls.
- *Don't accept a Saturday date after Wednesday.* Indeed, women can only yield to a man's furious activity under the strictest of circumstances. Again, within reason, this works. But nonsense such as the above is well beyond reason, in my opinion – not least because it removes a woman's autonomy.
- *Don't go Dutch on a date.* And they don't mean just the first date. No matter what a woman's status (compared to the man's), she's forbidden to contribute financially to the early stages of a relationship. Instead, she must act like a princess (or a 'creature unlike any other'), receiving the largess of the man as if she is his possession. Of course, many modern women will consider this a patronizing insult, although I noticed during my New

York dating days that this was the one 'rule' almost universally applied.

Be valued

To me, Fein and Schneider are looking down the wrong end of their presumably Edwardian telescope. They seem to be saying: 'be passive and make him do all the work – that way he'll appreciate you'. And being valued is, indeed, a key requirement for female confidence in the dating game. But precluding women from taking an active part in the relationship is – in my view – harming female confidence, not building it.

Instead, what *The Rules* should say to women (but only hints at), is 'take no shi*t'. In my view women should be active in pursuing the man they want. They can even make the first approach and – God forbid – pay for dinner. But any man should be under no illusion when it comes to your affections: he is extremely lucky to be in your company and, if he slips up, he's dead.

For instance, on an early date with my future wife I was tired, grumpy and less attentive than usual. She saw this as a sign I was taking the relationship for granted and simply walked out, saying she didn't want to see me again. I had to beg for forgiveness and behaved much better on future dates. On another occasion I insisted we walk somewhere rather than take a taxi: thrown again. A week later I committed another minor etiquette misdemeanour and was thrown over once more. On each occasion, my future wife was not playing games – she was interpreting my poor behaviour as a sign I was not valuing her sufficiently and she was therefore uninterested in the relationship.

Given this, I soon shaped up. Indeed, I began to value the relationship above all others: not because she didn't return my calls or expected me to pay for dinner – but because she had the presence of mind and, yes, confidence to refuse any form of mistreatment, no matter how minor.

My wife's behaviour in those early days taught me a major lesson with respect to my romantic dealings with the opposite sex, and it's one I pass on to all single women when dating: be as tough as hell. *Any* nonsense from a man – the slightest sign that he's disrespecting you – chuck him. If he begs for forgiveness, make sure he's learnt his lesson before you accept him back. And if he doesn't come back – well, you've saved yourself a great deal of potential misery and freed up your time for more profitable pursuits.

What's Stopping You Being More Confident? *For men, 'unattractive' attributes such as being short or 'ugly' can erode confidence with the opposite sex. They should instead avoid nightclubs and develop their personality. Women looking for sustainable relationships should avoid playing 'the rules' but should refuse any nonsense from men, forcing him to value the relationship or stop wasting her time.*

PART FIVE

Barriers

16

PREJUDICE

Prejudice exists. There's no denying it, some people will discriminate against you based on who you are rather than what you can contribute. And of all the barriers that can kill confidence, the suspicion of prejudice against us can be the most powerful. No other assumption so radically changes our behaviour – making us overly-sensitive and defensive and even causing us to behave in ways that confirm their perceived prejudice.

Most under-confident people have a version of this that plays out in stressful situations. These are often the very moments that can make the biggest difference to our lives – usually when we most need to impress – such as networking events, interviews or even social gatherings outside of our usual demographic. Yet the anxiety that such a situation generates heightens our sensitivities to signals – positive or negative – regarding how we're being judged, or pre-judged.

Race and gender are the two most obvious prejudices in this respect – followed by class, abilities, age, size, nationality, sexuality and, less obviously, beauty (or otherwise). Each can influence the way we're immediately perceived by others, making us overly-aware of being judged on those traits rather than on the 'content of our character', to use Martin Luther King's memorable phrase in his 'I have a dream' speech.

Suddenly, we're no longer just nervous in any given situation. We're mentally facing down what we perceive as condemnation based on our point of (usually-physical) differentiation. Of course, prejudice can work in our favour – perhaps with people that may judge our particular differences kindly (such as being a British male on the New York dating scene, as I found out). But in most cases we (rightly) assume the judgement is detrimental.

King's speech describes some of the most acute prejudice of the twentieth century – the appalling and officially-sanctioned discrimination endured by African-Americans in certain US states. And it's racial discrimination that perhaps sets the benchmark with respect to prejudice. To be an African-American at that time and in that place was to experience a depth of bigotry that must have weighed heavily on the external responses of those on the receiving end. Certainly, my earlier advice (about not assuming hostility) would sound ridiculous to an African-American girl in 1960s Mississippi – perhaps approaching a group of white men on a corner. Given the history of abuse and violence resulting from similar exchanges down the generations, responding with anything other than fear and distrust would have been imprudent. The perception of prejudice, in this case, had a strong grounding in reality – making any changes in behaviour a natural and protective response.

Prejudice is real

Yet that's the point about our perceptions of prejudice. They're often based on solid evidence, hence the fact we so profoundly change our behaviour when we perceive we're on the receiving end. Prejudice is real, and the instincts triggered are – in many cases – the right ones for our self-protection. We feel we're being attacked for who we are, and this can make us act in a distinctly defensive, unfriendly or even aggressive manner, which is a disaster for those looking to gain confidence through achievement.

My own version of this is based on a perceived class prejudice, which is as deeply-ingrained in the UK as race is in the US (if somewhat more subtle). As a lower-middle class boy 'educated' at an under-performing secondary-modern turned comprehensive school in the soulless housing estates of Essex, I found my accent and manners very different to most of my contemporaries at university. And while at university in the 1980s era of identity politics such differentiation was no bad thing – even something to accentuate – in the London media industry after university it led to feelings of prejudice despite being as well-qualified for the posts I applied for as anyone else.

Wide-eyed from what I saw as my strength (getting a good degree from a good university despite my poor secondary education) I stumbled into situations where I was, at best, patronized and, at worst, openly dismissed, humiliated and – yes – discriminated against: and this at institutions that held themselves up as bastions of liberal progress. Of course, this radically changed my behaviour. I lost confidence, quietened down and became defensive. And I guess I developed what privileged people like to call a 'chip on my shoulder' (an appalling expression that denies those on the receiving end of prejudice any legitimate expression of resentment regarding their ill-treatment).

Yet such 'chippiness' is a disaster for our confidence because it's a self-fulfilling admission of defeat. Sure, we have to fight a silent enemy that the guilty deny and the innocent find hard to conceive (and openly say so). But we can develop better responses when dealing with prejudice: ones that can mitigate the potential damage to our confidence rather than compound it.

Imposter phenomenon

A key need is to develop a self-awareness of the changes in our behaviour caused by the perceptions of prejudice against us. For instance, a crucial psychological basis for behavioural change is the phenomenon many call 'imposter syndrome', in which we feel we have no legitimate right to be in a certain group or place. And while much is written on the subject, two psychologists stand out: Pauline Clance and Suzanne Imes.

Their 1978 paper *The Impostor Phenomenon Among High Achieving Women* was the first to describe professionals – in this case women – who, having reached a significant intellectual milestone in their careers, fail to feel internally confident when with their peers, often due to feelings of being poorly judged by associates on the basis of their gender.

'They consider themselves to be 'impostors',' they write. 'Despite numerous outstanding academic and professional accomplishments, women who experience impostor phenomenon [they shy away from calling it a syndrome] persist in believing that they are really not bright and have fooled anyone who thinks otherwise. Numerous achievements, which one might expect to provide ample objective evidence of superior intellectual functioning, do not appear to affect the impostor belief.'

Imposter phenomenon, or 'IP' as the professionals call it, is therefore a self-fulfilling condition because our perceptions of prejudice cause us to develop poor self-judgements with respect to our suitability to be treated as an equal, which – in turn – leads to behaviour that may confirm such prejudice (i.e. we feel dumb so we start doing dumb things). And while IP was discovered in professional women, most psychologists now recognize it can impact anyone who communicates with apparent intellectual peers and yet feels insecure due to who they are, despite having earned their place through strong intellectual or academic achievements.

Tackling prejudice

So can the under-confident counteract the impact of IP and other behavioural changes brought about by perceptions of prejudice – especially if, as stated, prejudice is ingrained in our society? In my opinion, yes. Here are 10 steps that can prevent us being derailed by prejudice in social or interactive settings – with familiar themes repeated from previous chapters justified by my concern to tackle fully what I see as our highest barrier to confidence.

1. *Focus on what's changeable.* While the wider fight against prejudice is both legitimate and to be applauded, it belongs in what Stephen Covey (1989) calls our 'circle of concern' rather than our 'circle of influence'. This means that, while it obviously impacts our progress, it's beyond our control. It's important to acknowledge this and operate within your own 'circle of influence' – changing what you can change and ignoring what you can't. If you don't want to spend your life at war with those who can help you, this is an important mental compartmentalization.

2. *Don't give consent.* Think of Eleanor Roosevelt's famous quote: 'no one can make you feel inferior without your consent'. Of course, this is easy to say but less easy to feel. But you should nonetheless say it to yourself whenever up against perceived prejudice.

3. *Work out what you want.* If possible, aim to calculate beforehand what you want from any situation that may generate prejudice. What is your objective *here*? Then focus purely on achieving that objective. Every conversation should have this at the forefront of your mind, rather than any desperate calculations about how you're being received. This puts you on the front foot, regardless of who you're talking to. It will also help suppress those amygdala-triggering emotional reactions if you suspect bigotry.

4. *Bail out – if you want.* With your objectives pre-conceived for any interaction, you can now exercise the ultimate sanction: you can leave. Yet this must be a positive choice, not one exercised rashly. It must be judged against your objectives rather than your sensitivities. That said, it must also be mercenary. If there's nothing to be gained from an encounter with those who seem to dislike you for who you are, why hang around for the belittling? But don't walk away scowling at

the injustice. Walk away knowing that time spent with ignorant people is not just a waste of time, it's negative time.

5. *Dress conservatively*. If you're trying to be provocative, fine.
   But it's then a tad unfair to blame people for pre-judging you
   on your appearance. Signal your desire to fit in by dressing
   within the norms of any situation. In fact, go one step further
   – dress impeccably within those boundaries because it will
   broadcast your confidence.

6. *Get a line*. Echoing Chapter 12's idea about practising a story
   to help overcome timidity, prepare an opening line or two
   about who you are. Such lines are important aids as they
   explain your presence – giving you the initiative when trying
   to get to second base (the one that's a step beyond your
   race/gender/class) in any conversation. Your line should be
   a positive but not boastful description that states firmly your
   legitimacy. Avoid being defensive. And in the UK at least, err
   on the side of modesty. That said, beware of over-doing self-
   deprecation: given prejudices, it may be taken literally.

7. *Smile*. Yep, that old chestnut. Again, aim to look happy
   even if you don't feel it. Even if you're as nervous as hell and
   hating every minute – fake it. Sporting a scowl will confirm
   their worst prejudices, while seeing a smiling face will make
   everyone assume you're 'happy in yourself' and that you're
   worth knowing. Being funny is even better – but, again, don't
   go overboard, especially in a formal setting such as an interview. Don't forget, your aim is to be taken seriously, so
   providing wit and amusement is preferred to playing the
   clown.

8. *Put people at their ease*. There's just a chance that it's you
   pre-judging the situation – with *your* unease making *them*
   nervous. And there's an even bigger chance that it isn't discrimination that's being propagated, but their concern when
   talking to someone 'different'. They may feel they've nothing
   to say that could be of interest to *you*. So why not take the
   initiative and be interested in *them* – relaxing them by getting

the conversation on their ground? And could it be that their own insecurities are making them appear stand-offish when it's just nerves? It's a tough call, but it's absolutely in your advantage to assume so.

9. *Find a friend.* Prejudice can feel isolating (that's part of its intention). But anyone perceiving prejudice is unlikely to be alone. Seek out others that may be feeling the same way, although don't seek to recruit them. There's certain to be an unstated camaraderie between you, so expressing relief at finding someone 'friendly' is fine, but there are limits to this – not least because they may be uninterested in joining your gang (not wanting to become socially 'ghettoized'). Nonetheless, they should at least be welcoming, so a quick leveraging of the shared concerns is worth a try.

10. *Develop a kinder outlook.* Remember, all prejudice is ignorance. So we should develop a kinder view of their bigotry – it is, after all, them declaring themselves uninformed. Also, others are likely to have their own pressures and hierarchies to be concerned about, which may be driving their fears. In fact, there's a strong chance it's their lowly self-perceptions that are underpinning their prejudices – i.e. they feel threatened – even if they're acting as if in an exclusive club. Keep this in mind.

What's Stopping You Being More Confident? *Prejudice is real and can lead you to feel like an imposter, even when qualified for a position. Stay objectives-focused and remember that all prejudice is ignorance (often based on fear).*

17

PROCRASTINATION

While prejudice is an external force we have to navigate, procrastination is all our own making. Yet it's also one of the greatest barriers for the under-confident to overcome, not least when it comes to gaining confidence through achievement. Procrastinators are the people who delay execution until tomorrow, often employing valid-seeming excuses to justify their inaction. Yet the excuses are just that – invented delays that mask the real reasons for their repeated postponements.

'The emotional roots of procrastination involve inner feelings, fears, hopes, memories, dreams, doubts and pressures,' write psychologists Jane B. Burka and Lenora M. Yuen in their definitive book *Procrastination* (1983).

Burka and Yuen introduce the idea of the 'Procrastinator's Code': mistaken all-or-nothing thinking that ultimately destroys the procrastinator's ability to make progress. Statements under the Code can include:

- 'I have to be perfect', in which the procrastinator would rather avoid any form of execution than one risking imperfection
- 'Everything I do should go easily', in which the procrastinator cannot cope with even the smallest obstacle
- 'I must avoid being challenged', in which the procrastinator avoids competition for fear of humiliation

- 'It's safer to do nothing than to take a risk and fail', in which, again, the humiliation of potential failure is the main concern
- 'If I do well this time, I must always do well', in which the procrastinator fears being judged by the benchmarks they may be creating from their endeavour.

The judgement of others

Indeed, according to Burka and Yuen, it's the judgement of others that procrastinators fear most, although this can include the 'critic who dwells within'.

The mantra of the procrastinator therefore runs along the lines of 'you cannot mess up if you never try' or 'nothing ventured, nothing failed'. Many are perfectionists incapable of tolerating imperfection even as a stage in the journey. Others are control freaks who become obstinate when others ask them to perform. That said, many simply fear failure, and the public humiliation such failure will bring. In most cases, the procrastinator will mask their fears usually by adopting excuses – for instance, 'I started the project late, so I didn't have enough time' – which means they can continue to view themselves as capable individuals, just ones impacted by external factors (such as time) that prevented them performing to their potential.

'As long as you procrastinate you never have to confront the real limits of your ability, whatever these limits are,' says Burka and Yuen. For the procrastinator this can even extend to relationships in which they fear proximity or intimacy – perhaps employing unconscious tactics such as always being late in order to 'establish boundaries' with friends.

Parental influence

Unsurprisingly, the roots of procrastination are in childhood. Burka and Yuen cite parental influence, which can include heaping unrealistic expectations on a child, or making children feel like failures before even beginning a task. Of course, this carries over into adult life, with our brains hardwired into believing deep down we are incapable of accomplishment, hence the excuses – as well as the masks to preserve our fragile ego.

And it's such hardwiring that can explain why the procrastinator can become obstinate about small chores – even those others may find enjoyable. Again, the amygdala and hippocampus have combined to create painful associations that make the procrastinator appear, at best, irrational and, at worst, stubborn or lazy.

Given these potentially-deep psychological roots, how can you learn to defeat procrastination – or at least deal with it to prevent it becoming a major barrier on your journey towards confidence? Burka and Yuen suggest the following strategies (with some thoughts of my own):

- *Be analytical.* Emotions are vital for procrastinators because they're what drives their inaction, although this may not be obvious (and is potentially even suppressed). When they do surface it's usually unhealthily – perhaps stating 'I hate myself because I procrastinate'. Yet this can be substituted with more rational thoughts or questions, such as 'why do I procrastinate?' By using your diary to help unravel disabling emotions, it may be possible to induce a more analytical frame of mind.
- *Be realistic.* Low confidence is a core concern for many procrastinators (no matter how well it's hidden), which makes realistic objectives important. In this respect long-term goals are irrelevant because they contain a 'wishful thinking' or 'someday never' element – a classic procrastinator's indulgence that may allow action to be delayed. Getting the procrastinator out of their inactive funk, therefore, requires a focus on short-term objectives that can be clearly and quickly accomplished. Of course horizons can expand as these accumulate.
- *Understand difficulties in self-regulation.* Burka and Yuen are convinced goals are more likely to be attained when both mind

and body are relaxed. Certainly, for procrastinators, agitation is a problem because it blurs their focus and can lead to a breakdown (perhaps one conjured in order to remove the need to continue). Yet, for me, relaxation has its limits. I know procrastinators that could be accused of being too relaxed, or being too focused on their inner calm. Some frustration is therefore positive – acting as a strong signal that we should be making greater progress. So, as long as we can channel our frustration into directed action, being unrelaxed in mind and body is, within limits, acceptable: anything but one more day spent 'meditating' in front of the TV.

- *Deal with task aversion.* Disliking a task doesn't necessarily mean the procrastinator thinks it unpleasant. It could be their negative feelings towards the task that are generating an aversion to it, not the task itself. Again, by using your diary, you can get to the bottom of your emotions with respect to postponing a particular task due to some (potentially irrational) aversion. This may result, Burka and Yuen claim, in you even discovering your enjoyment of the task.

Tactics for the procrastinator

Yet I have my own thoughts on procrastination – or, at least, what's helped me get beyond it. These include:

- *Choose a positive goal.* 'Stop procrastinating' is a meaningless goal when analyzed, so avoid it. Instead focus on something positive such as 'finishing the marketing report by 1 June'.
- *Just get on with it.* Waiting until you feel like it or for this or that to be in place is simply making excuses: the Procrastinator's Code, no less. So just get on with it. Plunge in, despite the imperfect circumstances.
- *Calculate your first step.* It's a common problem – not starting because of not knowing what constitutes the beginning of your

endeavours. Why not write a letter to yourself outlining the problem? This classic cure for writers' block can also work for the procrastinator as it should mean that thoughts flow freely – helping to break that mental log-jam.

- *Establish work intervals.* One useful time-management tip invented by Italian Francesco Cirillo in the late 1980s is called the 'Pomodoro Technique'. Named after those ubiquitous tomato-shaped Italian kitchen timers, Cirillo states we should: (a) decide on the task to be done, (b) set the timer for 25 minutes, (c) work furiously on the task while the timer ticks off the minutes, (d) have a short break when the timer rings (including a small reward), and (e) reset the timer after five to 10 minutes.
- *Make a public commitment.* Friends, family, colleagues: you should declare your intentions to others so that you, absolutely, increase the potential humiliation of failure. As stated, the prospect of public humiliation is a strong demotivator for pro-crastinators, so by declaring your intentions publicly you've flipped it into a motivator (as you're now keen to avoid the embarrassment public failure will bring). And those that avoid declaring their goals? Well, maybe they're already preparing the ground for what they see as their 'inevitable' flunk.
- *Optimize your chances.* This simply states that your working environment is all-important. Find a work space that works for you with respect to task fulfilment, not against you. Certainly, I cannot write with the children playing around me or with the radio distracting me: I need to ensure I have a functioning and quiet workstation.
- *Expect setbacks.* Nothing goes smoothly all the time. Road-blocks and obstacles are inevitable. If you can accept them as part of the process – not as the barrier that will kill progress (perhaps the one you've been expecting since you started) then you'll be mentally prepared to prevent minor setbacks from reinforcing procrastination.
- *Reward yourself.* For the procrastinator, the aim is not to com-plete a task but to make progress, so why not set goals that

simply get you to the next break? I'll work until that morning coffee, nice lunch or even that afternoon nap – all involving that most vital of components for the procrastinator: the reward. Procrastinators cannot start a task because they cannot see the end (or see the stated end as realistic). So some self-delusion is required – in this case simply working for that next reward.

Ultimately, there's only one way to get beyond procrastination, and that's to take action. How you get yourself to that point is your choice. The only choice you don't have is to continue procrastinating – at least, not if you want to gain confidence.

What's Stopping You Being More Confident? *Procrastination has emotional roots, usually from childhood and often involving fear or pressure. Being realistic is important to overcoming procrastination, as is the establishment of a strong work pattern, with intervals and rewards. Ultimately, however, you simply need to be motivated enough to act.*

18

DEPRESSION

'Depression is a thief that steals from people, robbing them of energy, vitality, self-esteem and any pleasure that they might previously have enjoyed,' writes Dr Tony Bates in *Understanding and Overcoming Depression* (2001).

Bates calls depression the 'common cold of psychiatry', such is its prevalence, although it's also a condition often ignored by those needing help. Most suffer alone: perhaps isolating themselves by withdrawing from family or friends. Often it's triggered by an event such as losing a job or falling out with somebody close. But it's unrelenting – feeding on itself to generate a seemingly-permanent funk that destroys our confidence. Certainly, months of hard and constructive work in building our confidence can be wrecked by depression, which – as Bates states – is a 'profound psychological suffering that reduces a person's sense of physical well-being'.

Symptoms interrelate and include the following:

- *Thoughts*. For depressed people, thoughts are enemies, says Bates. We become constantly self-critical and hopelessly negative.
- *Feelings*. These include fear, guilt, anxiety and an almost total loss of confidence.
- *Physical changes*. Our sleep is disrupted, we lose appetite and our zest for life (including our libido) disappears.
- *Behaviour*. Children become disruptive, adults become irritable and impatient, or maybe inattentive or lethargic.

Obsessive negative thinking

Most important is what Bates calls 'obsessive negative thinking'. This is perhaps the most common sign that depression is upon us, not least because it cannot be eradicated and it destroys our confidence. That said, people experience depression differently. 'Dysthymia' is a low-level (even sometimes unnoticed) form of depression that lasts over a long period (perhaps months). Meanwhile, severe depressions last for at least two weeks and can even include suicidal thoughts. And then there's 'manic depression' or even being 'bipolar', which refers to mood swings from elation and hyperactivity to severe depression.

'What hurts most when you are depressed,' says Bates, 'is your compelling feeling that there will never be an end to your suffering.'

Of course, this feeling of hopelessness is both self-fulfilling and self-defeating. It's also a roadblock – destroying not only our progress but also our will to proceed. For it not to wreck our burgeoning confidence, therefore, depression needs to be tackled head on, and quickly. Depression is an enemy that we must fight aggressively, not least because passivity is its ally – reinforcing our gloom.

The causes

As expected, the roots of depression are in childhood. Negative early-life experiences can mean we develop a propensity for depression in adulthood. Neglectful, abusive or harsh parenting, traumatic events (such as the loss or rejection of a parent), or our poor treatment at the hands of siblings or peers can all set the ground for adult depression. According to Bates, these experiences lead many to develop 'rules for living' as a means of controlling our lives (similar to those for low self-esteem, as noted in Part One). For instance, if we are rejected as a child we may unconsciously adopt the rule that 'to feel good about myself, I must make sure I'm liked by other people'. Of course, this is a rigid rule that's certain to be broken on occasion – even by strangers in a shop or restaurant. And this will knock our self-confidence and lead to feelings of depression.

And there's no escaping the fact depression can be caused by biochemical changes in the brain or neurochemical imbalances. Early-life conditioning can create such changes, although they can also be genetic or 'evolutionary', suggesting – according to Bates – that some people are more 'genetically sensitive' to depression than others, although this also makes them more treatable through medication.

Guilt and depression

That said, Bates insists that 'it's not your fault you are depressed', although feelings of guilt are not so easily dismissed in my view. Indeed, for me, guilt is a major part of feeling depressed: that somehow it's me causing the negativity around me – making my downer feel self-induced and therefore no more than I deserve.

Certainly, for the under-confident, depression is as much a response to negative events as their cause. Tiny incidents can unsettle our fragile 'up' state, potentially throwing us into freefall where feelings of depression are the first mental ledge we grasp in our descent. And I mean tiny incidents. Just yesterday in a coffee bar I thanked a member of staff for calling my order when it became ready – a change in behaviour in an establishment that usually leaves uncollected orders to go cold (hence the 'thank you').

'I *did* call it,' she snapped, thinking I was being sarcastic.

Yet rather than see this as the café's guilty conscience regarding their previous poor service, I became emotionally-triggered and therefore incapable of a logical response – instead interpreting this as *my* fault: perhaps me projecting negative vibes via my 'thank you'. Within minutes, the chemicals in my brain had done their job and feelings of depression began washing over me – flooding my thoughts for the rest of the day.

Pathetic, yes? Certainly so, but you may well recognize such reactions, as well as understand the desperate need to fight these feelings as they develop.

Slaying the internal monster

Bates talks of 'defeating depression' and I think such embattled imagery correct when depressed. We've been taken over by an internal monster that must be slain. Far from a silly approach, such imagery is important because it forces us to realize depression is an imposter. As Anthony Robbins states in his seminal work *Unlimited Power* (1987), some people assume depression to be their natural state. Extraordinarily, some depressives can even find depression comforting – perhaps helped by secondary gains such as sympathy from relatives or allowances from peers.

For anyone seeking confidence, however, such defeatism is a disaster. And by embracing the imagery of a knight slaying the depressive monster (or any other suitably violent metaphor), we are at least fighting back. That said, we must also divide our tactics into those that kill our current depression and those that prevent depression from returning.

Below I list some of my preferred tactics for beating the blues, remembering that – as Bates points out – severe depression is a clinical condition requiring professional help.

1. *Know that it's temporary.* As stated, depression can become an indulgence. It can also lead to self-reinforcing behaviour such as drinking too much or playing melancholic music. Sure, wallow in your despondency – after all, any bungee-jumper or sky-diver can tell you that falling is a pleasant sensation. But, soon enough, the bungee rope kicks in or the parachute opens. So also be aware that this mental descent can be no more than a temporary extravagance.
2. *Note the positives.* Having spent 10 minutes feeling like a loser, now spend another 10 minutes forcing yourself to note

the positives, no matter how meagre they feel or how refutable they seem. Health, friendship, family, income – the fact you're alive and therefore tomorrow's coming – anything. Just note that, within the doom, good fortune exists. Write it down (in the usual place).

3. *Note the problems.* Keep with the writing for a moment, because it may help to also write down your misfortunes. Why do they feel like such a calamity? What went wrong? Where was the wrong turning? And what are the lessons that can prevent a repeat? Certainly, if I'd written earlier about that small incident in the café some perspective would have kicked in, making it less disruptive.

4. *Plot your steps to redemption.* There's always a second chance. Sure, you may think not, but I thought that after the 'failure' of my first book and here I am writing my third! That said, it took me 10 years to write my second, which I now consider a self-inflicted waste. I thought there was no way back – a notion you must refute in the strongest terms. So why not plot the steps required to make that second chance a reality, however unlikely it now seems?

5. *Plan 10 years hence.* There's no need to repeat this one, although it's worth noting that the very process of planning so far in advance can mentally lift you from your current state: helping convert seemingly irrefutable pessimism into cautious optimism. After all, will you still be depressed in a decade's time? *Really?* Indeed, in many cases our current despondency is no more than impatience or frustration, both of which are – when correctly targeted – positives. So use planning to reset your compass and, once heading in the right direction, note the progress.

6. *Maintain your routine.* While depressed, it's important to maintain a routine no matter how hard that seems. Go to work, visit your parents at the weekend, keep that date with a friend. Assuming you're bad company and withdrawing is a colossally self-reinforcing move. Sure, you may be bad

company for a few minutes, but so what? Most people enjoy hearing others' misfortunes (within limits), because it makes them feel empathetic. Also, keep getting dressed, keep washing, shaving and – especially – exercising (and if you don't exercise, go for a long walk or bike ride – or just visit a museum). Life isn't a movie, so it's ridiculous to try and look and act the part as well as feel it.

7. *Break the routine.* No, I'm not contradicting myself. Find room to add another dimension. Haven't been to the cinema for years? Then go (but choose a comedy). Never seen an opera? Do so. Always wanted to learn how to ride? Now's your chance (though realize it will require practice). Invest in your happiness.

8. *Be nice to strangers.* Don't project your depression onto others through irritability or bad manners, especially with respect to strangers. If you usually say good morning to the security guard, force yourself to keep doing so. Their positivity will radiate back. But so will your negativity if it's stronger. So be false: maintain the veneer. It may just produce a moment that shatters the pain.

9. *Give something up.* Sugar, caffeine, cigarettes, chocolate, meat, pornography, trashy novels, TV, alcohol, pot-smoking, fatty foods: anything that doesn't add to your long-term well-being. Just *one* thing – I'm not asking you to become a monk. Dumping something bad for you will immediately make you feel better, reframe your negativity (because you've achieved a small victory) and distract you from your current misery.

10. *Donate to charity.* Something small but significant: £10, perhaps. And don't discriminate with respect to the cause (or you'll potentially reinforce negative feelings). Why not give £10 to the first mainstream charity box you find? After exercise, nothing triggers the release of endorphins more readily than a charitable deed. And don't look for a 'thank you'. In fact, do the opposite: just this once, make sure no one knows you've done it. This is your small, private, victory

against what Winston Churchill called the 'black dog' of depression.

Prevention rather than cure

Sure, such tactics may help arrest your downer. But how do you employ longer-term tactics that prevent the blues from returning? As stated, you may be genetically disposed towards depression, making its eradication impossible (a condition that requires clinical help). But you can still improve your defences when trying to prevent it taking hold.

Here are some suggestions:

- *Self-awareness*. This is both a short-term and long-term need. We can find ourselves in a continuous loop of negative thoughts, criticism, self-loathing and depression. This is a cycle that may have previously been resolved in one of two ways: by spiralling down to the bottom before slowly picking yourself up, or by waiting for positive external events to reverse the spiral. Yet both are destructive because both remove your autonomy. Instead, you must become self-aware: analyzing what caused the downward fall, identifying your perhaps irrational reactions, recording what Bates calls 'negative automatic thoughts' and listening to bodily reactions such as a racing heart or adrenaline rush. Just being aware of what's happening to you – and why – can help break the cycle.
- *Work on your self-esteem*. As stated in Part One, under-confident people often have low self-esteem. And this is also a major long-term cause of depression. Low self-esteem and depression are negative bedfellows – and you cannot fight one without concern for the other. Again, a growth mindset is crucial, as is reframing negative thoughts and language.
- *Build your network*. Never cut yourself off from others, no matter how tempting it feels at the time. Certainly, this is a

favourite of mine – a 'sod it, I'll become a hermit' reactivity when triggered. As stated, depression can feel like a permanent state. So to reinforce that feeling by removing ourselves from any form of sociability is madness. Instead, we should do the opposite: try and extend our network of associates, no matter how false this can feel in the initial stages.

- *Reduce stress and anxiety.* For me and many others, stress and anxiety are regular triggers for feelings of depression, which makes reducing stress and coping with anxiety vital requirements. So vital, in fact, the next chapter is dedicated to the subject.

What's Stopping You Being More Confident? *Depression is 'obsessive negative thinking' that can remove your confidence and destroy your willpower. Its roots are in childhood – and they are not your fault. Yet depression can be defeated through self-awareness and a focus on the positives. A growth mindset is also vital.*

19

STRESS AND ANXIETY

Interestingly, stress is the one malady under-confident people happily confess. When pushed to the limit, when stretched beyond endurance, when simply unable to cope, we'll openly state that we're stressed – and may even seek treatment. Yet such a confession is often the wrong way round. Stress is not the cause of our problems. It's a symptom.

Until recently, I assumed stress had dogged my entire adulthood, and certainly my career. When confronted about my poor behaviour or my mistreatment of others – or simply about a regrettable response – I've readily blamed stress over any other trait or concern.

Indeed, the phrase 'sorry [add name], I've been very stressed lately' is one of the most common confessions to leave my lips.

But in each case I've been wrong. Such behaviours are the classic reactions of the insecure. And it's my insecurities that generated my stress – a realization that, in my opinion, must come before all others when trying to cope with stress. For the under-confident, stress is not a cause of our problems: it's another negative result.

Pressure greater than our ability to cope

Of all the definitions of stress, the best for me came via a short course (in coping with stress) held at the Bishopsgate Institute in the City of London.

'Stress,' said the woman running the course (after drawing a simple set of scales on a whiteboard), 'is when we think the pressure upon us is greater than our ability to cope.'

She then drew a second set of scales, this time up-ended by a weight on one side. This is a mental image that returns each time I feel the adrenaline coursing through my body or the blood rushing to my hands, or any of the other 'fight-or-flight' signals that tell me, yet again, I'm stressed.

The truth of this mental imagery has been a more recent realization, however, with my previous ignorance caused by my disregard of a key element of the stress counsellor's statement (which she helpfully wrote on the board beneath the sketched scales). Like many other stressed people, I'd glossed over the words 'we think' – assuming that everyone will experience stress when pushed too far. But it's our evaluation of our capacity to cope that matters, which is why others cope with pressure while the under-confident succumb.

Appreciating the moment

So what can be done to alleviate stress? Of course, there are lots of books and courses on the subject – not least because (thanks to it being a condition we're happy to confess) they sell well. After all, buying a book with the word 'stress' in the title suggests we're busy people with lots of responsibilities. But most of these books offer little beyond common-sense observations about exercise, relaxation, diet and – at best – desensitization, in which we turn any task into a series of small steps (as with courage in Part Two). This is the world of the 'power nap' and camomile tea: refined sugar, bad; complex carbohydrates, good; deep-breathing exercise, good; phone-slamming and hair pulling, bad.

You get the picture.

Is there a better way? Well there is 'mindfulness', which takes the common sense recommendations of the de-stress professionals to their logical ends. It's the vegan version of the vegetarian diet on offer in all those books. At least that's what I thought – based on my preconceived prejudices whenever anyone mentioned the word. Certainly, few things used to irritate me more than a meditating hippie eating lentils while tantric chanting in the lotus position – and that's where I visually landed when 'mindfulness' was mentioned. But that's the insecure, stressed person talking: the one annoyed by the thought of someone else being at peace while I'm at war, although we both occupy the same space – coping (or not) with the same issues.

Maybe the hippie can teach me something after all, if only I'd stop long enough to listen.

In fact, that's the point – mindfulness is an appreciation of the present moment. And it's that thought – no more – that drives the Buddhist concept of meditation. This sounds simple. And the concept, at least, is. Mindfulness is an awareness of *now* – it's paying attention to what's going on: being awake, alive, engaged. Yet it's the flipside of being stressfully distracted, which can be exciting but also – as we know – tense, traumatic and unhealthy.

Mindfulness isn't an awareness brought about by sensory overload but by sensory underload. For instance, kayak a set of rapids and we're full of energy: our attention is heightened, our observation sharpened. Time appears to speed up as we navigate the river's rocks and channels – cutting a path through the rushing water while avoiding the many dangers. Yet sit on the riverbank and closely observe a single rock, and the opposite happens. Time slows as we watch the water bubble, the sun glint and the rock stand motionless in the stream. It's the same spot – yet it's a totally different perspective. And it's one worth adopting when stressed.

'The best way to capture moments is to pay attention,' writes mindfulness practitioner Jon Kabat-Zinn in *Wherever You Go, There You Are* (1994), the book now considered a classic on mindfulness and meditation. 'Meditation does not involve trying to change your thinking by thinking some more. It involves watching thought itself.'

The uses of mindfulness

Extraordinarily, this makes mindfulness – and even meditation – useful to the under-confident: not in some life-changing become-a-Buddhist sense, but in the very practical ways it suggests we evaluate the world around us. In fact, much of it isn't so far removed from the advice already peppering these pages:

• *Patience.* This is a pointless virtue unless exercised at the very moments we're most prone to losing it. Mindfulness here – mentally getting out of the kayak and sitting on the riverbank – can be transformative.
• *Non-judgement.* Another crucial need, not least when we're at our most judgemental (usually when stressed). Whether we're right or wrong, the very act of judgement (especially of others) clouds our view, removes our autonomy and ramps up our stress. By making no judgements at all, therefore, we're reducing our stress.
• *Generosity.* Stress makes us mean when we most need to be generous. For the mindful, meanness of spirit is intellectual poverty, which will reinforce the pressure upon us, while mental generosity embodies us with wealth – a notion that should surely help alleviate the tension. Particularly when angry with someone, this single change of stance can temper our stress.
• *Humility.* Far from revealing weakness, humility makes us stronger. It's pomposity and defensiveness that makes us weak, not least because we're trying to defend some brittle sense of self. Humility, meanwhile, goes with the flow. It's flexible – preventing humiliation, and therefore opening our world to stress-free risks.

- 'Voluntary simplicity.' We should not speed up, but slow down. We should not add complexity but seek simplicity. We should not search for more but instead see more: all by forcing a focus on our core needs while jettisoning peripherals.

So, whether or not you choose to adopt the lotus position and burn incense, the above is sound advice for getting beyond your stress. And I'm not even disparaging their call for less meat and no caffeine: I'm sure it all helps, although not as much as simply taking a moment to be 'in the moment'.

Anxiety – a natural state

Killing anxiety, however, requires more than mindfulness. Worry really does seem to be hardwired into us. It's a survival mechanism, rooted in our very instincts as animals once part of the food chain. Our nervous system requires us to be alert to danger – triggering fight or flight responses when seemingly threatened by predators. And while such responses now seem inappropriate, their leftover sense of concern seems to fit nicely into a modern world full of stress, complexity and uncontrollable forces.

Certainly, the under-confident tend to fret, sometimes perhaps without knowing why. And when gripped by fear, we become incapable of action. We invent potential catastrophes that play out in our imagination like disaster movies – scaring us rigid or forcing us into panic and retreat.

Anxieties can be reactive: perhaps triggered by phobias or irrational fears. But they can also be a nagging discomfort, or even just low-level feelings of confusion. Of course, moderate levels of anxiety are motivating. The fear of being unable to pay the bills, or of being left behind while our peers excel, can gel us into action. Fear can help us plan for future events (such as retirement) and can even improve our immediate abilities (adrenaline sharpening our reactions). In fact, anxiety can even be fun – for instance, at a fairground – all of which can perhaps be explained by the fact humans are animals addicted to progress, which makes some level of anxiety inevitable: even desirable.

'Humans are not content when they reach homeostatis, or equilibrium, at which all pressures are absent,' writes C. Eugene Walker PhD in *Learn to Relax*, his 1975 book on coping with stress and anxiety. 'They are most content or happy, and life is most meaningful, when they are responsibly meeting and solving problems.'

In fact, this is good news for the under-confident – or at least those concerned enough to want to do something about it. Our anxiety is an expression of our desire to make progress: it just worries us. This is a positive feeling. But there's a line we cross where our enabling fears – perhaps those solving problems – become disabling. Excessive anxiety adds problems, potentially invented ones, and destroys our performance, even at basic tasks. It can cloud our judgement, reduce our skills and kill our motivation.

This requires attention, which – as with stress – means we must change our viewpoint. Indeed, according to Walker, a key source of anxiety is the way we interpret our experiences. It's not the event that makes us uneasy, but our interpretation of it.

NLP and anxiety

This is an area where NLP can help. Worrying tends to have a pattern, notes Ian McDermott in *Boost Your Confidence with NLP* (2010): both in how it starts and how it proceeds.

'When you're worrying, you often create a narrative,' he writes. 'It's the story we tell ourselves that generates the feelings.' He asks us to ask ourselves:

* What triggers worry in you?
* What are the stories you keep rerunning?
* What are the recurrent themes?
* What changes your state so you stop worrying?

According to McDermott, some 'worry narratives' are realistic, though most are not. And, he says, worry can easily become a habitual state, particular if not challenged. And this can be a precursor to depression, which – as we have seen – will wreck our confidence. So tackling it early is an important requirement.

McDermott offers seven steps (with some thoughts of my own):

1. *Do a reality check*. What exactly do I fear, and is this realistic?
2. *Think again!* Watch for habitually negative thinking that spirals downwards. Maybe you're in a repetitive pattern of thinking that needs breaking – perhaps by switching attention elsewhere.
3. *Stop obsessing!* McDermott recommends the technique of 'thought stopping' – literally crying 'stop it!' (a step best taken in private).
4. *Breathe.* Fear constricts breathing (perhaps because our primeval instincts were to hide from predators), so remember to take deep breaths.
5. *Exercise.* It's a cliché, but exercise can burn off excess adrenaline and release endorphins, therefore generating feelings of well-being – even if temporary ones.
6. *Be generous.* Focusing on others is a low-cost antidote to the self-absorption of anxiety.
7. *What's safe?* Calculate what constitutes safety or comfort. Then mentally calculate the steps towards achieving it. Such a plan should offer a mental haven – like knowing the fire escapes in a vulnerable building. That said, it may only work if it's achievable, so you may have to be prepared to enact your plan.

Yet we can sometimes feel overwhelmed by anxiety, such is the enormity of our trouble. Here, McDermott suggests two further strategies. First, we should look for an element within our concern where it's possible to exercise *some* control: anything to reduce the aching helplessness that can erode the worrier's well-being. And, second, ask yourself whether you're prepared to 'let go' – freeing the path in front of you by simply deciding to 'know that you don't know'.

'Given that we cannot control the world, we might as well learn to control our fears,' says McDermott. 'Being able to realistically assess the threat, take steps to address it and then change your internal state so that you can once more be master of your fate is an extraordinarily empowering thing to do. It does wonders for your confidence!'

What's Stopping You Being More Confident? *Stress is when you think the pressures upon you are greater than your ability to cope, a common problem for the under-confident. Relief comes through mindfulness – i.e. being 'in the present moment'. Anxiety, meanwhile, is a survival mechanism, and based on the human need to grow as humans.*

20

HUBRIS

Around the year 2000 I went on several dates with a professional woman. By the third date, however, she'd had enough. She'd decided I was too cocky and I needed taking down a peg or two. She spoke out, telling me I was 'arrogant, over-confident and full of it'.

Yet this intended insult produced an instant and genuine response that she wasn't expecting.

'Thank you,' I said. 'That's the nicest thing anyone's ever said about me.'

Indeed, I bristled with pride. After all those years of being under-confident – of loathing my inability to feel, see and do the right thing because of the insecurities that hijacked my rational brain at every turn: forcing me into, at best, shyness and, at worst, angry defensiveness – someone was insulting me for the opposite trait. I was delighted.

But this was far from a happy ending in terms of my journey towards confidence. In reality, this was a total derailment. Over-confidence or hubris is a disaster. It's the flipside of the confidence coin but one no more effective despite its shiny outward appearance. We're no further along in terms of confidence because our under-confidence has been replaced with something far worse: stupidity.

Hubris flatters to deceive. We're perpetrating a lie against ourselves: claiming excellence when, in reality, we're racing off a cliff made all the higher due to our pumped-up vanity. We still have no control over our confidence. Indeed, we remain as insecure as ever, just an insecure person hiding behind a veneer of arrogance. Sure, we may have had some success – hence the vanity. But, such is the depth of our insecurity, we're determined to project that pathetic success on to everyone we meet.

This is a fool's paradise. It's failure in a fur coat – not least because, having failed to learn the lessons, our confidence will almost certainly be snatched back, potentially without us even knowing why.

Enron – hubris on an epic scale

Don't believe me? Still think success is all that's required – perhaps with a sprinkling of manufactured public humility so we don't come across as too loathsome? Yes, so did I, which – in my case – was unforgiveable: not least because I'd witnessed first-hand the monumental devastation hubris can unleash.

As a US-based banker in the late 1990s my favourite client was Enron, the gas-pipeline owner turned international multi-utility turned über-trader. They were involved in every area of interest to my world – from receivables finance, to project finance to securitization – making them my potential saviour as I struggled for deals in the tough North American market.

Everyone I met at the company's Houston headquarters glowed with confidence and cheer. I'd never visited a place of work that felt so happy, so brimming with smiling people, so engaged, so pleased to greet me and shake my hand and meet my gaze. From the security guards, to the receptionists, to the executives – the skyscraper was bursting with potential. It was as if neat oxygen was being pumped in through the air conditioning, such was the air of expectation that pervaded those vast workspaces in the sleek, organic curves of the Enron Centre.

Everyone I met at Enron felt like they were at the top of their game, making our banking teams look like amateurs in comparison. They dressed well (though in the 1990s corporate casual male uniform of chinos and a Ralph Lauren polo shirt) and spoke fluently, no matter how complex the subject. In fact, I became amazed at the depth and breadth of their knowledge – it was hypnotizing. These guys (a collective term that included the minority of female executives) were the most talented people I'd ever met, working in a building that seemed to harness that talent and reward it fully: no wonder everyone was smiling.

Yet this was *Alice in Wonderland* for MBAs (with apologies to Lewis Carroll). It was a land of make-believe in which every one of the power-hungry 'talents' on the other side of the meeting room table had fallen down the rabbit hole and was now working alongside the Mad Hatter and the March Hare, though had yet to realize their fate.

The worship of talent

In fact the fantasy, which was almost entirely built on accumulating vast amounts of cheap debt in order to muscle into immature markets by overpaying for assets, lasted about a year after my departure from banking in early 2000. Even in my meetings, the talk was of structures that helped remove some of their mountains of debt – concerned as they were about their credit rating. Indeed, they hoovered up our modest plans for off-balance sheet receivables structures, as well as anything else that allowed them to park debt away from the parent company.

We were too entranced to heed the warnings, although in retrospect they were glaring. Far from suspecting the company's fragility – hence their keenness to seduce small-time trade financiers working for an unfashionable UK bank – we too adopted the smile and walk of those allowed into Wonderland.

Yet from 2000 onwards the company suffered a series of losses that impacted the fragile state of many of their off-balance sheet debt vehicles. And in 2001 Enron collapsed, destroying 20,000 jobs directly (and many more indirectly) in what was then the largest corporate bankruptcy in history.

'Enron did a fatal thing,' writes Carol Dweck in *Mindset* (2007). 'It created a culture that worshipped talent, thereby forcing its employees to look and act extraordinarily talented.'

Dweck uses Enron as one of several examples when trying to explain the causes and consequences of a fixed mindset: she concludes that over-confidence forced Enron's employees into a fixed mindset in which they had to demonstrate financial omnipotence. Everyone within the company was forced to act and sound like the 'smartest guys in the room' to use the title of Bethany McLean's famous book on Enron's collapse (2004). There was no space for humility, or of being 'work-in-progress'. They had to believe they were the finished article: intellectual gods, no less.

For instance, this is Dweck's view on the CEO (including her italics): 'As resident genius, [Jeff] Skilling had unlimited faith in his ideas. He had so much regard for his ideas he believed Enron should be able to proclaim profits as soon as he or his people had the idea that might lead to profits. This is a radical extension of the fixed mindset: *My genius not only defines and validates me. It defines and validates my company. It is what creates value. My genius is profit, Wow!*'

Of course, this worked – especially on under-confident bankers desperate for deals. That said, it also worked on Wall Street analysts who were accused of 'just not getting it' when questions were raised. But in truth Skilling and his cohorts were engaged in pure hubris. They were losing all contact with reality due to the corporation's collective arrogance and pride. Enron was riding for the most almighty fall in corporate history – a spectacular implosion of a company I feel privileged to have witnessed firsthand simply to be able to say I've seen what hubris on such an epic scale looks and feels like, as well as results in.

A seductive elixir

In fact, what it feels like is seduction. Over-confidence is an intoxicating elixir that you hope will never run out: hence the broad smiles at Enron. But it's also enticing you into a trap, in which each challenge is met – not with an open mentality and the need for learning and correction (a growth mindset in other words) – but with deceit as you attempt to stay 'up'. Lie piles upon lie, until your confidence is so brittle – and brooks so little challenge – that the very discovery you most fear is almost certain to smash over you like a breaking tidal wave.

According to management consultant and academic Matthew Hayward writing in *Ego Check* (his 2007 book on executive hubris) over-confidence manifests itself in four overlapping qualities that combine to create a toxic mix. And while Hayward is concerned with corporate America, they make enlightening reading for individuals trying to cope with confidence for the first time:

- *Acting based on excessive pride.* Perhaps becoming too concerned by your external image, you cannot be seen to exhibit any weakness or culpability.
- *Not seeking or receiving external help (or even opinion).* Of course, this could be a result – like Skilling – of assuming no opinion is more valid than your own, although it may be your inner fear of being contradicted (or having your insecurities revealed).
- *Failing to evaluate reality properly.* This can include being unconcerned by the risks involved in any particular action – even finding the risks addictive.
- *Failing to face the consequences of a mistake.* Pride before a fall, as they say, but only after mistakes have been hidden – generating further deceit until the entire edifice comes crashing down (as with all those 'rogue trader' financial scandals that begin with small early losses being covered up).

Business people regularly lose perspective when it comes to confidence, says Hayward. Many fail to balance the confidence they need to succeed with the danger of an overbearing ego once they get too full of themselves. He cites Apple's oscillating history of success, failure and then a return to success as a manifestation of Steve Jobs pride. The company's initial success was destroyed by ego-related mistakes such as the refusal to cooperate with Microsoft. Yet Jobs learnt from that mistake and spent his second period in charge of Apple building alliances, even overcoming his aversion to 'all things [Bill] Gates related', says Hayward.

Avoiding hubris

Is hubris therefore unavoidable for those climbing the ladder of confidence, at least until the lessons of over-confidence have been learnt? Is it something that can only be viewed in retrospect, after the fall? Not always, although humility is certainly a key lesson at that point.

To avoid hubris, Hayward recommends the following steps (adjusted to be relevant for individuals):

- Consider the consequences of every decision before moving ahead
- Make sure your decisions are good for your wider world (business, family, friends), as well as yourself
- Be consistent in your behaviour and choices (perhaps using your long-term goals as a benchmark)
- Focus on getting the job done rather than positioning yourself to impress senior management
- Discount plaudits from those with ulterior motives (such as salespeople)
- Share any praise with others that helped – instantly and completely

- Separate your compensation (i.e. money) from your sense of pride
- Avoid embellishing or exaggerating your abilities
- Don't assume you have crossover abilities – having gained strong competence in one area
- Make sure your 'pride' is grounded – i.e. that it's reality-based.

The joy of the SWOT

Of course, the above is easy to write but less easy to execute. Certainly, if these were the cardinal rules for avoiding hubris, I'd have failed every one of them: not once but many times; not in the distant past but also recently. For the under-confident to remain grounded once they have achieved some level of success – after a lifetime of poor results and dashed hopes – feels like an impossible, even unjust, task.

Yet, as we have seen, hubris kills confidence and destroys achievement. It's also a false feeling – making our best bet the injection of some form of structural process that's not only focused on retaining humility but also allows us sustainable pride in our progress. And the best process I can think of is the SWOT: the generation of a document that records our strengths, weaknesses, opportunities and threats.

At Moorgate we undertake SWOTs at the beginning of every PR campaign, although it amazes me the number of times our clients struggle to think of weaknesses or threats: some even becoming defensive when we offer suggestions. Yet it's important to realize that everyone has elements of themselves for every one of the SWOT's headings. And if you think not – you just haven't looked hard enough.

But the SWOT should never be seen as a barrier to progress. It's an aid, pointing out where we can act immediately (our strengths), where we should try and improve (our weaknesses), what areas should be our focus for progress (the opportunities) and what may prevent progress (the threats). And, importantly, the SWOT needs to be a dynamic document, which means it should be executed regularly – perhaps when we swap diaries at the beginning of each year (which is when we also renew our long-term goals). Only then will we be able to see that our strengths are accumulating, as are the opportunities, but that this very process throws up new and different weaknesses and threats.

And if you get so 'full of it' you cannot think of a single weakness or threat? Under weaknesses you should write 'ARROGANCE/ STUPIDITY' in giant letters and under threats you should write 'PRIDE BEFORE A FALL'. That way, you'll know you're in the danger zone – and can do your best to avoid it by re-evaluating.

Those that struggled to win confidence may read the above and conclude they're immune from such needs, the struggle alone being enough to inject humility. Yet it's not. In fact, it's more likely to render them arrogant: not least because, as discussed, their insecurities haven't been eradicated, and have potentially developed into an ugly and preening vanity.

Ultimately, become an entrepreneur

Yet, in my opinion, there's one way of guaranteeing our confidence doesn't stumble into hubris. It's the ultimate route to sustainable but grounded self-confidence: start your own business. Given the swashbuckling and fearless image of the entrepreneur, however, I should explain. Contrary to popular belief most people who work for themselves are not vainglorious egotists trying to take over the world: usually via some Steve Jobs or Richard Branson 'screw it, let's do it' throw of the dice. They're simply trying to start a sustainable enterprise resulting in them no longer having to work for somebody else.

Many entrepreneurs will have what they see as a talent or skill in a particular area – a specialist self-efficacy usually built up, as we have seen, from high levels of endeavour and serious investments in time. And this inevitably results in them wanting to explore this talent, not for a boss or big company, but for their own account. Of course, this can be within a major corporation or institution (although acting autonomously). But, most likely, it will be for *Me Inc.* or *Me Ltd.* – somewhere (even if just a bedroom or shed) with our own nameplate on the door.

They'll need optimism to do this, and some courage. But they'll also need caution. While confidence in yourself can help you take that first step towards career autonomy – covering (or at least being aware of) of the downside risks is also a vital component of entrepreneurism, which makes judgement and trust important attributes when generating and executing the long-term plans required for venturing alone.

The self-efficacy of the self-employed

Yet if starting a business requires a modicum of confidence to get going (though usually one assisted by strong planning), that's nothing compared to the confidence generated from working for yourself. Ever wondered why the window cleaner whistles, or the London cabbie is so happy to offer his unsolicited views on the world – or even why the white van driver appears so cheeky? It's because they have no one to answer to. Within reason, they can do and say what they please.

Indeed, it's worth observing any entrepreneur because, in my view, three things become obvious. The first is that they work extremely hard. The second is that, despite this, they seem happy. And the third is that they ooze confidence. Not the fragile but preening confidence of the powerful, which is what leads to hubristic behaviour. But the quiet confidence of autonomy, which comes from the fact they're making a living from their own efforts. They have achieved Maslow's self-actualization and their self-efficacy in a particular area is fully employed *for them*. What's more, they have

Dweck's growth mindset at the front of their mind – always – because they have to remain on top of their game while also seeking opportunities to expand.

If you're still doubtful, compare this with the confidence of those within a formalized hierarchy: perhaps in your company or in politics. Notice the uneasy sense of power they exude – of commanders interpreting the orders of others while attempting to retain authority over their charges. Also notice their need for the baubles of achievement: the job title, the office, the car, the business-class flights – anything that publicly advertises their fragile power. And notice their behaviour: not the inner strength of those with autonomy but that disturbed and edgy sense of fleeting supremacy.

Confidence by this route is, in many cases, not confidence at all. It's under-confidence in a better setting, which may look like a great result but is unlikely to increase your well-being because the stakes are higher and the stress more acute: little wonder the result is so often the false paradigm of hubris.

Of course, the stress of entrepreneurialism is also real, but then at least it's matched by real and sustainable confidence. Over-confidence, meanwhile, is structurally eradicated because running your own business requires clients, and (in most cases) staff, whose support you need – usually without the rewards others can offer. Yes, there are lots of potential clients and a seemingly endless pool of labour: and there are entrepreneurs that seem happy with the 'scorched earth' approach of burning through staff and customers through arrogance or petulance (perhaps via a 'creative temperament'). But their ventures are unlikely to prosper to the scale of their potential (though they may be happy with this). At the very least, they prosper *despite* such attributes, not because of them.

For us, however – with our core need of developing strong confidence – such masking is unacceptable. We need sustainable, deep confidence. And that requires Dweck's growth mindset, which is confidence capped with humility. It's the ability to know what we don't know, and be more than willing – eager, even – to learn. To defer to others, and to enrol them in our pursuit of personal growth.

And that may be the final point about confidence. It's not a big office or a new car or a bigger house: or even the admiration of those we seek to impress. It's self-acceptance – knowing yourself and being happy with the results such knowledge generates. This is not a leap with respect to your circumstances. But it is a perception leap with respect to how you regard yourself. As the Zen saying states: 'Before enlightenment I chopped wood and carried water; after enlightenment, I chopped wood and carried water' – although the confident person can perhaps add 'yet this time I was whistling'.

What's Stopping You Being More Confident? *Hubris or over-confidence is a fool's paradise and, in reality, no more than a disguised form of under-confidence. It can also lead to disaster. The SWOT can help you to avoid hubris, although the best cure is to maintain a growth mindset and accept yourself as work-in-progress – always.*

THE ROUTE
TO CONFIDENCE –
IN SEVEN STAGES

Stage One: Examine why you are under-confident

Perhaps events in your childhood gave you negative self-beliefs, or maybe you were naturally more introverted than those around you? You should also examine each of the key relationships in your early life: parents, siblings, teachers and peers. What scripts emerged in those key relationships? Did anyone undermine your confidence at this stage – perhaps by being overly-critical or by favouring a sibling or peer? Were you misunderstood or disliked, or perhaps rejected or humiliated?

Stage Two: Calculate the impact of this on your present thinking

How do the scripts that emerged in those early relationships now play out? Are they repeated in your dealings with others? Do you have a role that you always fall into (the criticizer or pacifier, maybe)? Is this role based on negative self-beliefs that were formed from our interactions with others when young? What behavioural traits in adulthood can be traced back to those key

221

primary relationships: defensiveness, timidity, defeatism, with-drawal, fear, anxiety, anger, even depression?

Stage Three: Understand the alchemy of confidence

Observe confident people around you. What traits do they possess? Do they have a self-belief in their attributes? Are they motivated, optimistic, outgoing? Do they have good judgement? Are they trustworthy and able to get on with people? And are they resilient – able to cope well with setbacks? Also, can they plan ahead and take action without hesitation or rumination? This is the alchemy of confidence, with each trait something that can be learnt and adopted, no matter how false it now feels.

Stage Four: Focus on where you want to gain confidence

Nobody is confident in all things: we have to discriminate. In what area of your life is it most important for you to gain confidence? Is it a leisure activity (perhaps a sport) or (more likely) something in your career? If so, is it in your current career or in a completely new direction? What interests and motivates you enough to see you through those early setbacks? At this stage you need to think of positive goals that you want to achieve rather than negative goals, or things you want to run away from (such as your current poor status).

Stage Five: Plan for confidence

Confidence is never gained in one giant leap. Confidence in any-thing involves a series of mostly-predictable small steps. You need to know what these steps are – in as much detail as possible. And you need to calculate ways of achieving those steps. Focus is required, but so is a strong idea of the big picture: of your destination. Within your desired zone, you must know what confidence looks and feels like. And you must calculate the steps required, as well as know how to take them.

Stage Six: Act

Create the mental and physical space in which to act. And then do so – recording your progress in a daily journal. If you succeed, learn the lessons and plan for the next small step. If you fail, think about why and apply the lesson by trying again. And then repeat – never assuming that you cannot improve, or that you've 'made it'. No matter what the success, humility remains crucial if you are to avoid a self-defeating hubris. And no matter what the failure, we can learn the lesson and show resilience: after all, instant confidence in anything is a myth.

Stage Seven: Become confident when dealing with people

Other people are the gatekeepers of your confidence because they provide the feedback you require. You need to become effective in dealing with people: overcoming shyness through good preparation, by not assuming hostility and by focusing on their needs and their feelings, rather than your own. Certainly, you should become aware of the impact you have on others – and develop grace and tact at all times. Importantly, you must avoid having a fixed mindset in which you are constantly trying to prove your worth. Instead, develop a 'growth mindset' – in which everyone is there to teach you something.

This is a book from the heart: about my own experiences as an
under-confident person, as well as the efforts I've made – intellectu-
ally and physically – to get beyond my insecurities. Yet what about
the head? Where does all this sit within the established world of
psychology? I'm no psychologist (I'm a curious sufferer), but below
– to add some context – I outline the relevant milestones from the
great and the good of that world.

Sigmund Freud (1856–1939) – and the unconscious mind

Of course, we must start with Freud, the godfather of psychoa-
nalysis. It's the unconscious mind that fascinated this Austrian
neurologist. He thought it the essential element of the mind for
explaining how we perceive and experience reality. Crucially –
although it contains all our memories, thoughts and feelings
(generating our sometimes irrational reactions) – it's also beyond
our control, and even our awareness.

Freud, together with Vienna contemporary Joseph Breuer, popularized psychological treatment based on the notion that past
traumas can generate irrational fears, paranoia, anxiety and hyste-
ria. Their claim was that the release of repressed memory from the

unconscious mind allowed patients to confront that experience and set free trapped emotions.

The two parted after disagreements regarding the sexual origins of psychological ailments, but the breakthrough into the unconscious mind had been made. In Freud's view, the active state of consciousness – the operational mind that we're aware of – is just a small fraction of the mental forces at work. He spoke of three realms of consciousness: the conscious, the preconscious (what isn't conscious but isn't repressed) and the unconscious (perhaps painful and thus repressed memories that nonetheless dictate our behaviour).

For Freud, painful thoughts could be diverted away from the conscious and into the unconscious mind (what he meant by 'repression'). We repress traumatic childhood memories (perhaps of abuse) or unacceptable desires (perhaps of a friend's spouse), although their power remains manifest. Indeed, the unconscious mind drives our instinctive behaviours, including our reactions when threatened.

Alfred Adler (1870–1937) – and the inferiority complex

Freud's view was limited to the unconscious, while another Vienna contemporary, Alfred Adler, expanded this to include conscious influences, including external social and environmental factors. Adler was the man that invented the inferiority complex, being fascinated by the positive and negative impact of self-esteem on our psyche.

Feelings of inferiority are universal, he considered. All children are born inferior because they're surrounded by larger, stronger, more capable people. Yet this inferiority motivates them to improve, with contrasting results for the psyche. In some, success relieves the feelings of inferiority. For others, it doesn't: resulting in an inferiority complex as well as feelings of low self-esteem.

Most difficult to shift are inferiorities brought about by physical differences. If we're smaller than our peers, uglier, fatter or in any other way different, we may develop a generalized notion of inferiority, which leads to an imbalanced personality, says Adler. In these cases, feelings of inferiority are never relieved.

A key fascination for Adler was the effects of physical disability on achievement and the sense of self. He found large differences between disabled people, some of whom had achieved high levels of athletic success while others felt defeated and made little effort to improve their situation. Self-esteem was the key divider, Adler concluded.

Carl Jung (1875–1961) – and archetypes

Jung expanded upon Freud's unconscious by delving into its elements and workings. Myths and symbols from highly individual and geographically disparate cultures were nonetheless strikingly similar, he noted, leading him to assume they shared a common psyche: a 'collective memory'. Layers of inherited recollection went back to the dawn of existence, thought Jung, and have created 'archetypes': personality types or templates within our own psyche that interpret our personal experiences.

Archetypes are inherited emotional and behavioural patterns that divide humans into groups with similar traits and outlooks. Each type will contain elements that are part private and part public, part conscious and part unconscious. It also has both masculine and feminine elements and can be both moral and immoral.

To Jung, what feels like instinct is our unconscious use of archetypes. These fill the gaps in our individual knowledge with a pre-existing substructure of inherited experiences that have a tremendous impact on our perception of events.

Jung assumes self-realization is the essential goal of human existence: the archetype of the 'true self'. This is an organized and harmonized character that seeks enlightenment, although Jung claims it can only be found by those that consciously seek it.

Karen Horney (1885–1952) – and the 'shoulds'

All social environments develop cultural norms, said German psychoanalyst Karen Horney. And these undermine our self-determined beliefs. This 'toxic' environment leads to two influences in the psyche: the 'real self' and the 'ideal self' that's dictated by cultural 'shoulds' such as 'I should be thin' or 'I 'should be outgoing'. The 'ideal self' fills the mind with inappropriate goals that generate negative feedback for the 'real self'. And this creates a third self: the unhappy 'despised self'.

Fritz Perls (1893–1970) – perception shapes reality

Perls was a founder of Gestalt therapy, a precursor to cognitive behavioural therapy (CBT) in which the complexity of the human experience is seen through the 'lenses' of the individual – meaning that we scan and select from all the influences and images that flood our world. Our reality is therefore no more than perception, and experiences are never absolute truths but simply our own viewpoint of an event.

Perls was rebelling against what he saw as the 'rigid' psychoanalytical norms of the 1940s, in which patients were at the mercy of their unconscious until 'saved' by an analyst. We can change our own reality, said Perls, by encouraging personal growth via an internal sense of control – consciously pursued regardless of our external environment.

The 'why' is not important for Perls, with respect to our insecurities. It's the 'how' and 'what' of our responses that matter. The use of language is also critical to the therapy – changing 'can't' statements to 'won't', for example, in order to emphasize that we have a choice.

Under Gestalt therapy our actions are tools, which can then be used consciously to change reality. There are two layers: how we interpret the environment and how we respond. For instance, that Eleanor Roosevelt quote – 'no one can make you feel inferior without your consent' – is a classic example of Gestalt therapy in action. We are responsible for how we act and react, and even feel.

Erich Fromm (1900–1980) – 'know thyself'

Humans are defined by the need to find meaning in their lives, says German-American psychoanalyst Erich Fromm. Life is painful, he said, but it can become bearable though the pursuit of our authentic self, the discovery of which allows us to 'love life'.

Humans live in a state of struggle because we're constantly trying to balance our individual needs with our desire to connect, said Fromm. We want to live at one with nature and with others, yet we can perceive ourselves as separated from nature and isolated from others, which has the capacity to make us miserable. In Fromm's view, our ability to reason separates us from nature, but makes us aware of our isolation: creating tension, anxiety, loneliness and hopelessness.

To overcome these negative feelings we seek connection with others, which – in turn – means we conform to group norms, an approach Fromm considers misguided. For Fromm, it's important to discover our individual self rather than hand responsibility for our choices over to convention or authority. Indeed, the very purpose of our lives is to define ourselves by embracing our 'personal uniqueness'.

Many people invest time and money cultivating a self that others will accept – perhaps via fashion or material wealth or by joining the right club. Yet this is futile, says Fromm, as only a person with a strong sense of self can stand firmly and give freely to others. If you're oriented towards receiving love – rather than giving it – you'll remain insecure and fail, said Fromm. Your autonomy is lost, because your needs are external, and therefore beyond your control.

Carl Rogers (1902–1987) – and the person-centred approach

American Carl Rogers became hugely influential due to his criticism of mid-twentieth century psychological practices, which he thought too rigid to account for the full human experience. For Rogers, mental well-being is not a fixed state that's suddenly achieved by following a specific programme. Instead, a healthy 'self concept' is a fluid and open-minded entity capable of change.

There's no 'self-actualized' destination (as with Maslow) in which we are fully adjusted, said Rogers. In fact, that's not the purpose of existence, which is to grow and to discover without destination (until death). An essential ingredient is the ability to stay 'in the moment'. To enjoy the experience and remain open to the possibilities – allowing the experience to shape the self. This means we must trust ourselves – taking responsibility for our choices and developing an 'unconditional positive regard' of ourselves and others.

If we hold onto our ideas of how things *should* be, rather than accepting how they *are*, we'll perceive our needs as mismatched against the available choices, which will cause conflict, defensiveness and unhappiness. We can even find ourselves denying or distorting what's happening in order to defend our preconceived ideas, said Rogers. To counter this we must be open to new experience and be completely without defensiveness.

As with Carol Dweck's 'growth mindset', Rogers' openness requires a perception leap. Yet the alternative is to feel alienated from the world around us – 'a square peg in a round hole', says Rogers – perhaps raising barriers or conditions that must be met before we accept ourselves or approve of others.

Viktor Frankl (1905–1997) – suffering ceases with meaning

Holocaust survivor Frankl wrote that humans have two psychological strengths allowing us to endure painful situations and move forward: the capacity for decision and the freedom of attitude. No matter what our circumstances, we're not at the mercy of our environment because we can shape our response, perhaps giving meaning to our suffering. He used an example of a man's grief for his dead wife. Asked to consider her feelings if he'd died first, the patient could see that she'd been spared the grief he now felt, which made his pain endurable. 'Suffering ceases to be suffering at the moment it finds meaning,' said Frankl.

Albert Ellis (1913–2007) – and irrational thinking

Rational beliefs create healthy emotional reactions, said US psychologist Ellis, a man viewed as an early influencer in the popular adoption of CBT. His own version – Rational Emotive Behaviour Therapy (REBT), or Rational Therapy, which predates Beck's work – asserts that experiences do not cause specific emotional reactions. Instead, it's the individual's belief system that prompts such reactions. People and things do not upset us. Rather, we upset ourselves through believing that we can be upset by people and things.

So while we can gain insight by examining our childhood, our symptoms will remain because the need is to focus on the way a person thinks *now*. Irrational people draw extreme conclusions that are usually negative. Yet, according to Ellis these are illogical, damaging and self-inflicted. Meanwhile, rational thinking is helpful because it's based on tolerance and our ability to deal with stress without assuming catastrophe. Losing your job doesn't mean you're worthless: it's simply an event, potentially even a positive one.

Ellis was influenced by the 'tyranny of thresholds' – Karen Horney's notion that something *should* be the case. Meanwhile, rational thinking focuses on the acceptance that 'stuff happens'. Yet it's also about taking control of our responses. Our problems are our own, meaning that we control our own destiny. If we take time to consider a response (rather than respond 'automatically' and probably irrationally) we'll be able to explore the 'infinite possibilities' each event presents.

Virginia Satir (1916–1988) – the family 'factory'

The 'Satir Model' is hugely-influential in psychology because of its family-centric approach to self-esteem. Partly formulated from her own experiences when growing up with an alcoholic father on a Wisconsin farm, Satir assumed dysfunctional families descend into individual roles that shape the child's personality into adulthood.

A healthy family involves open and reciprocal displays of affection, as well as expressions of love and an unconditional mutual regard. The power of this compassion nurtures well-adjusted people, with the opposite the case when such compassion is absent. Meanwhile, dysfunctional families (that display no mutual compassion) damage the potential for well-adjusted adult personalities.

Such families often fracture into identifiable 'roles', of which there are five, according to Satir:

- The 'blamer', who constantly finds fault and criticizes
- The 'computer', a non-affectionate intellectual
- The 'distractor', often the youngest child, who stirs things up
- The 'placator', often the mother, trying to please everyone
- The 'leveller', often the oldest child, who's open and direct.

Other than the leveller, the roles reveal degrees of low self-esteem, as well as a need to hide their true feelings of unworthiness. They can also overwhelm the true self and be disabling for adult relationships (not least due to the obvious connection with Oliver James' 'scripts' – see Part One).

Healing, said Satir, requires that each family member accepts self-worth as a birthright, which should start the journey towards honest communication (previously the sole realm of the leveller) and the fostering of compassionate relationships. For Satir, love and acceptance is the most potent healing power of all, although this may have to be sought elsewhere – the roles in existing family structures potentially being too entrenched.

BIBLIOGRAPHY

Adler, Alfred. *Understanding Life: An Introduction to the Psychology of Alfred Adler*. Oxford: Oneworld Publications, 2009.

Bandura, Albert. *Self-efficacy: The Exercise of Control*. New York: Worth Publishers, 1997.

Bates, Tony. *Understanding and Overcoming Depression*. Freedom, CA: Crossing Press, 2001.

Benun, Ilise. *Stop Pushing Me Around!* Franklin Lakes, NJ: Career Press, 2006.

Blanchard, Ken. *One Minute Manager*. London: HarperCollins, 1983.

Briers, Dr Stephen. *Brilliant Cognitive Behavioural Therapy*. Harlow, UK: Pearson Education, 2009.

Burka, Jane B. and Yuen, Lenora M. *Procrastination*. Cambridge, MA: Da Capo Press, 1983.

Cairo, Jim. *Motivation and Goal-setting*. Franklin Lakes, NJ: Career Press, 1998.

Carlson, Richard. *Don't Sweat the Small Stuff at Work*. London: Hyperion, 1998.

Carnegie, Dale. *How to Win Friends and Influence People*. New York: Simon & Schuster, 1936.

Carnegie, Dale. *How to Stop Worrying and Start Living*. New York: Pocket Books, 1948.

Carnegie, Dale. *How to Develop Self-confidence and Influence People by Public Speaking*. London: Vermilion, 1957.

Caunt, John. *Boost Your Self-Esteem*. London: Kogan Page, 2002.

Cirillo, Francesco. *The Pomodoro Technique*. Raleigh, NC: Lulu.com, 2009.

Clance, Pauline and Imes, Suzanne. *The Impostor Phenomenon Among High Achieving Women*. Atlanta, GA: Georgia State University (academic paper), 1978.

Clarkson, Petruska. *Gestalt Counselling in Action*. London: Sage Publications, 2004.

Clarkson, Petruska and Mackewn, Jennifer. *Fritz Perls*. London: Sage Publications, 1993.

Colvin, Geoff. *Talent is Overrated: What Really Separates World-Class Performers from Everybody Else*. London: Nicholas Brealey Publishing, 2008.

Covey, Stephen. *Seven Habits of Highly Effective People*. New York: Simon & Schuster, 1989.

Covey, Stephen. *The 8th Habit*. New York: Simon & Schuster, 2004.

Coyle, Daniel. *The Talent Code: Greatness isn't Born. It's Grown*. London: Arrow, 2010.

Diagnostic and Statistical Manual of Mental Disorders. Washington, DC: American Psychiatric Association, 2000.

Dweck, Carol. *Mindset*. New York: Ballantine Books, 2007.

Ellis, Albert. *Overcoming Destructive Beliefs*. Amherst, NY: Prometheus Books, 2001.

Ellis, Albert and Harper, Robin. *A Guide to Rational Living*. Englewood Cliffs, NJ: Prentice Hall, 1961.

Fein, Ellen and Schneider, Sherrie. *The Rules*. New York: Grand Central Publishing, 1995.

Fennell, Melanie. *Overcoming Low Self-esteem*. London: Constable & Robinson, 1999.

Frankl, Viktor. *Man's Search For Meaning*. London: Ebury Publishing, 1959.

Fromm, Erich. *The Art of Loving*. London: Unwin Books, 1962.

Fromm, Erich. *The Art of Being*. London: Constable & Robinson, 1993.

Gladwell, Malcolm. *Outliers: The Story of Success*. New York: Little Brown & Co., 2008.

Gladwell, Malcolm. *What the Dog Saw*. New York: Little Brown & Co., 2009.

Goleman, Daniel. *Emotional Intelligence*. London: Bloomsbury, 1996.

Goleman, Daniel. *Working with Emotional Intelligence*. London: Bloomsbury, 1998.

Gregory, Richard L. (ed.). *The Oxford Companion to the Mind*. Oxford: Oxford University Press, 1987.

Gross, Richard. *Psychology: The Science of Mind and Behaviour*. London: Hodder Arnold, 2005.

Hallowell, Edward M. *Shine*. Cambridge, MA: Harvard Business Press, 2011.

Hayward, Matthew. *Ego Check*. New York: Kaplan Publishing, 2007.

Hoffman, Edward. *The Drive for Self: Alfred Adler and the Founding of Individual Psychology*. Cambridge, MA: Da Capo Press, 1997.

Horney, Karen. *Neurosis and Human Growth*. New York: Norton, 1950.

James, Oliver. *They F*** You Up*. London: Bloomsbury, 2002.

Janov, Arthur. *Primal Therapy*. London: Abacus, 1990.

Jeffers, Susan. *Feel the Fear and Do it Anyway*. New York: Fawcett Columbine, 1987.

Johnson, Paul. *Churchill*. New York: Penguin, 2010.

Jung, Carl. *The Archetypes and the Collective Unconscious*. New York: Routledge, 1991.

Kabat-Zinn, Jon. *Wherever You Go, There You Are*. New York: Hyperion, 1994.

King, Paul W. *Climbing Maslow's Pyramid*. Leicester, UK: Matador, 2010.

Kluger, Jeffrey. *The Sibling Effect*. New York: Riverhead Books, 2011.

Lakhani, Dave. *Persuasion: The Art of Getting What You Want*. Hoboken, NJ: John Wiley & Sons, 2005.

Lee, Gus. *Courage*. San Francisco: Jossey-Bass, 2006.

Maslow, Abraham. *A Theory of Human Motivation*. Washington, DC: Psychological Review (journal), 1943.

Maxwell, John C. *Talent is Never Enough*. Nashville, TN: Thomas Nelson, 2007.

McDermott, Ian. *Boost Your Confidence with NLP*. London: Piatkus, 2010.

McLean, Bethany. *The Smartest Guys in the Room*. New York: Penguin, 2004.

Olsen Laney, Marti. *The Introvert Advantage*. New York: Workman Publishing Co., 2002.

Paul, Richard W. and Elder, Linda. *Critical Thinking*. Harlow, UK: Prentice Hall, 2002.

Plous, Scott. *The Psychology of Judgement and Decision Making*. New York: McGraw Hill, 1993.

Rachman, Stanley. *Fear and Courage*. New York: W.H. Freeman & Co., 1989.

Reina, Dennis S. and Reina, Michelle L. *Trust and Betrayal in the Workplace*. San Francisco: Berrett-Koehler, 1999.

Robbins, Anthony. *Unlimited Power*, London: Simon & Schuster, 1987.

Rogers, Carl. *Client-centred Therapy: Its Current Practices, Implications and Theory*. Boston, MA: Houghton Mifflin, 1951.

Satir, Virginia. *The New Peoplemaking*. Palo Alto, CA: Science and Behavior Books, 1988.

Seligman, Martin E.P. *Learned Optimism*. New York: Vintage, 1990.

Solomon, Muriel. *Working with Difficult People*. Upper Saddle River, NJ: Prentice Hall Press, 2002.

Steinhouse, Robbie. *How to Coach with NLP*. Harlow, UK: Prentice Hall Business, 2010.

Stevens, Anthony. *Jung: A Very Short Introduction*. Oxford: Oxford University Press, 2001.

Storr, Antony. *Freud: A Very Short Introduction*. Oxford: Oxford University Press, 1989.

Storr, Anthony. *The Essential Jung: Selected Writings*. Princeton, NJ: Princeton University Press, 1993.

Strachey, James. *The Standard Edition of the Complete Psychological Works of Sigmund Freud*. London: Vintage, 1999.

Strauch, Barbara. *The Secret Life of the Grown-up Brain*. London: Penguin Books, 2010.

Style, Charlotte. *Brilliant Positive Psychology*. Harlow, UK: Prentice Hall, 2011.

Sullivan, Paul. *Clutch: Why Some People Excel Under Pressure and Others Don't*. New York: Portfolio, 2010.

Sweet, Corinne. *Change Your Life with CBT*. Harlow, UK: Prentice Hall Life, 2010.

Syed, Matthew. *Bounce: The Myth of Talent and the Power of Practice*. London: Fourth Estate, 2011.

Taylor, Ros. *Confidence at Work*. London: Kogan Page, 2011.

Walker, Eugene C. *Learn to Relax*. Harlow, UK: Prentice Hall, 1975.

ABOUT ROBERT KELSEY

In 2011 the Capstone imprint of John Wiley & Sons, Ltd published *What's Stopping You?*, a book exploring why smart people often fail to reach their potential. This was Robert Kelsey's first successful book after what he perceived as the failure of his debut book, a lad-lit comedy detailing his life as a British investment banker in New York. Indeed, that book – *The Pursuit of Happiness* – was written to explain Robert's perceived failure as a banker: one selling highly toxic financial products to the likes of Enron.

Notice the word 'perceived' in the above descriptions. In both cases it was Robert's self-beliefs that condemned his pursuits as failures – resulting in actions that, indeed, confirmed that status. Oddly, this is the reverse of what happened in his previous career. As a financial journalist, Robert had developed a preening arrogance regarding his rather modest attributes – largely due to the flattery of those seeking to influence his articles. This resulted in hubris, and the over-reaching of his capabilities via his disastrous foray into investment banking.

The link between these career disasters and the success of *What's Stopping You?* is Robert's noble attempt to research and explain his insecurities. He concluded that behind every career and academic disaster, as well as every seemingly-unsustainable success, lay his deep lack of confidence. He also realized that his early-life experiences were trapping him in a cycle of low self-esteem – generating either low-attainment (further knocking his confidence) or modest attainment (resulting in hubris and near-certain disaster).

Finally, there was Robert's modest pursuit as an entrepreneur: using his knowledge of both finance and financial journalism to create Moorgate Communications, a specialist public relations company. Learning from a previous entrepreneurial experience (unsurprisingly ending in failure) – as well as his intervening addiction to self-help books (and the psychologist's couch) – Robert visualized and planned a future that reflected his values and leveraged his skills and experiences. The result: a sustainable achievement, which helped improve his confidence while preventing hubris.

What's Stopping You? Being More Confident is the second in Robert's series of books on the insecurities that wreck the careers and lives of otherwise highly intelligent and seemingly very capable people. Having overcome his phobia of public speaking, he also gives the occasional talk on the subject. He lives with his wife and two boys in London and Suffolk.

INDEX

Index

Index

Index